God *and the* Spiritual Tsunami

God *and the* Spiritual Tsunami
Responding to Revelation

KJELL AXEL JOHANSON

Foreword by Ola Hossjer

RESOURCE *Publications* • Eugene, Oregon

GOD AND THE SPIRITUAL TSUNAMI
Responding to Revelation

Copyright © 2018 Kjell Axel Johanson. All rights reserved. Except for brief quotations in critical publications or reviews, no part of this book may be reproduced in any manner without prior written permission from the publisher. Write: Permissions, Wipf and Stock Publishers, 199 W. 8th Ave., Suite 3, Eugene, OR 97401.

Resource Publications
An Imprint of Wipf and Stock Publishers
199 W. 8th Ave., Suite 3
Eugene, OR 97401

www.wipfandstock.com

PAPERBACK ISBN: 978-1-5326-5340-7
HARDCOVER ISBN: 978-1-5326-5341-4
EBOOK ISBN: 978-1-5326-5342-1

Manufactured in the U.S.A.   06/21/18

Scripture quotations are from The ESV® Bible (The Holy Bible, English Standard Version®), copyright © 2001 by Crossway, a publishing ministry of Good News Publishers. Used by permission. All rights reserved.

To Vivi-Ann

Wife, best friend, and supporter

…it is written…

Contents

Foreword by Ola Hossjer | ix
Thank you | xi
Introduction | xiii

Chapter 1
Premise 1: God—We Can Know that He is Here | 1

Chapter 1b....
Follow-up: A Look at Paul's Letter to the Romans | 11

Chapter 2
Premise 2: Sin is Our Problem but God Does Not Leave Us | 17

Chapter 3
Follow the Signs—Israel | 31

Chapter 4
Follow the Signs—The Church | 46

Chapter 5
Follow the Signs: Turning Persecution to Victory | 58

Chapter 6
Follow the Signs: The Bible—A Reliable Record | 72

Chapter 7
The Tsunami and What to Expect: Change | 84

Chapter 8
**The Tsunami and What to Expect:
Revival in the Muslim World** | 105

Chapter 9
**The Tsunami and What to Expect:
Israel's Conversion and Our Response** | 117

Foreword

The last decade the world has witnessed a political and religious turmoil that few of us would have anticipated some years ago. Wars and military threats in the Middle East, international terrorism, and persecution of Christians have all reached new levels. In the midst of this tsunami, Christianity is spread faster than ever at most continents, and most recently in the Muslim world. In addition, more Jews than ever are returning to their homeland Israel. Is it even possible to understand what is going on, or is all this just an unpredictable chaos? The world is shaken, and we are all looking for answers. For this reason, this is such an important book, where Pastor Kjell Axel Johanson guides the reader and shows how many of the Biblical promises from the Old and New Testament are coming true today, and will continue to do so in the near future. In fact, we live in a most exciting time, where the evidence for the Bible is stronger than ever. But in order for us to understand this we have to read the Scripture with open eyes. Kjell Axel Johanson helps us to do just that. He carefullly explains how God the Creator has spoken to us through the Bible, and how we are called to have a relationship with Him through Jesus Christ, as vice-rulers of the world. It is not until then we get a proper perspective and understanding of what is going on in the world. For this reason, I would highly recommend this very topical book to Christians and non-Christians alike.

Ola Hossjer
Professor of Mathematical Statistics,
Stockholm University

Thank you

Vivi-Ann Johanson for your time investment, encouragement and beautiful curiosity

Inger Lannero for reading, editing, praying for and believing in this project

Marta Johanson Radwan for reading this with your loving, smiling but eagle eyes

Mike Clarkson for taking so much time to proof read, comment and suggest ideas

Bruce Collins for always being so encouraging, giving positive critique and insight

Kerry Shook for giving me the opportunity to try my wings with these ideas at the Woodlands Church

Introduction

GET READY FOR A TSUNAMI

Early Sunday morning, December 26, 2004, a powerful tsunami swept over coastal areas in Asia. More than 200,000 unsuspecting people perished, among them 543 Swedish tourists who had chosen to seek sun and warmth over Christmas in Thailand.

Years before, Minister Dayalan Sanders had built an orphanage on Navalaji Beach on the Eastern Sri Lanka coastline to save children from the civil war that had plagued the island for many years. Early this Sunday morning Pastor Sanders was preparing for a church service in his bedroom when his wife burst in with a look of horror on her face. She told him the whole sea was rushing in. When Dayalan looked out he saw a wall of water approaching. In his own words: "It was a massive 30-foot wall of sea. . . black in color, stretching from one end of the beach to the other end of the beach and the very sight of this mass of water rushing towards us—it was like a thousand freight trains charging at you—that thunderous roar itself petrified you with fear." Without having any time to think, he called to all the children and staff – all 32 of them – to get into their boat by the lagoon. It usually took them over ten minutes to get everybody into the boat but now it took them just under 10 seconds. The motor was in place on the boat—they always took it off every evening—but this morning, and on this day only, it was already on the boat. They pulled the rope to the motor and it started—also a first. Starting the motor usually took several

Introduction

attempts. With the motor running, Dayalan then did two things exactly right: First, he decided to steer the boat straight towards the wave, to try to make it to the crest. Second, as they were "eye to eye" with the wave, a verse from the Bible popped into his head and gave him an idea. Summoning all his courage, he stretched out both his hands and spoke to the wave: "I command you in the name of Jesus Christ and on the strength of the Scriptures, to stand still!"

Something remarkable happened (also reported by villagers who were watching the boat while desperately clinging to nearby palm trees): it looked as though something held the wave back; it stood still for a few seconds and then slowed down. Although all the buildings on the orphanage campus were flattened by the power of the waters, everyone in the boat was saved—not one soul from the orphanage lost. The reports from eyewitnesses and the stories of journalists who followed up on the story later confirm this account.

The story illustrates two principles in this book. There is a God who acts today. There is also a cultural, political and religious metaphorical tsunami gathering power under the surface of ordinary world events, and, when it is released, it will turn the world as we now know it upside down.

Perhaps we have already begun to sense some of what is coming. Recall the recent political situations in USA, Britain, Greece, France, Italy, Venezuela, Russia, North Korea, the Middle East and the Philippines – right across the world. The chaos we see today was unimaginable twenty years ago, and regardless of what particular political ideology you subscribe to, I'm guessing you don't like what you're seeing. An unstoppable tsunami is approaching. I want to show throughout this book there is a story behind this—it is the most important story of all time—and it helps us understand what is happening and why. The story also guides us to know how to navigate our lives at this time in history.

It might come as a surprise to some—though it is a well-documented and well-studied phenomenon—that the growth and dynamic of the Church is creating a spiritual and cultural landscape

Introduction

that excites millions, while literally putting the fear of God into millions of others. One of the most powerful Christian movements today takes place underground in Iran, and there are signs that a similar thing is happening in Afghanistan. It's easy to imagine why the Iranian Mullahs and the Afghan Taliban are upset and desperate.

Thousands upon thousands of Muslims become followers of Jesus Christ in the Middle East and North Africa every day, exasperating radical Islamist groups. I think I can understand their frustration: they believe they serve God and try to honor Him while the supposedly Christian West, on the surface, does not even seem to make the attempt. Yet, many around them are turning to this God 'of the West'. But perhaps they fail to realize that the West no longer attempts to represent the God they once worshipped. True, Christians are still living more or less freely in the West, but the culture in the West boasts of being secular and promotes lifestyles that are not even remotely Christian. In fact, there is now a huge divide between Christianity and Western culture and values. Case in point: in Europe it is probably as difficult to be an open Evangelical or traditional Roman Catholic Christian in political leadership as it is in Indonesia! You cannot find many Christians today in the West who still evangelize in the streets, but those who do are sometimes arrested and taken to court for challenging other's beliefs. Even in the traditionally most Christian nation in the world—the USA—senator Bernie Sanders publicly opposes Evangelical Christians being appointed to top government positions, and liberal politicians and government sponsored think tanks in the US and UK work on how to help Christian leaders to re-interpret the Bible to be more in line with current societal values.

On the other hand—and here comes another surprise—many of the Muslim dominated countries are today moving towards an expression of historic Christianity with an intensity and power that few countries in the West have ever seen. If you have never thought in terms of the difference between Christendom (governments and church upholding each other) and Christianity (the

Introduction

Christian faith expressed in the great variety of churches throughout the ages) then what goes on in the world-wide Church must look terribly confusing. Watchful Christians have, however, always suspected that a time with seeming chaos would arrive. And I, for one, am convinced of this. What is going on will seriously disrupt the cherished way of life that cultures on all continents boast of. Jesus called this "birth pains" and there is no better word for it. Its benefit is that it can help us become as prepared as Jesus called people to be.

But before we get that far, I want to begin this book by affirming some essential, key puzzle pieces many Christians secretly from time to time have doubts about. The pieces we must lay for the picture to emerge are: 1) There is a God and the belief in God is a moral and not an intellectual question. 2) God created mankind out of His goodness as His representatives on Earth. 3) Since God is by nature good and generous, the essence of sin is to doubt this goodness and walk away from Him. 4) God nonetheless continues to seek man in order to bless him, and He has an encompassing plan to accomplish that purpose. He began this purpose through His covenant with Abraham and is fulfilling it through Jesus Christ. 5) Contemporary evidence of this purpose can be seen clearly in what He is doing right before us: We see it in the nation of Israel, through the growth of the Church and the persecution of the Church.

It is ironic that the very pressure on the Church designed to get it to deny the truth of God's power, involvement and goodness, will forge a faith of high caliber in many—no diamond was ever shaped without pressure.

But before this makes you want to run a mile, remember that nothing will stop God's plan to bless as we approach the time of the great tsunami—the turbulent time of upheaval of existing structures as God shakes the earth awake. There will neither be violence nor arrogance from true believers. The very opposite will be true: we can expect violent attempts from both extreme religious groups as well as secular groups to stop this movement, much like what we see in the book of Acts. But ultimately, what happens is not the

Introduction

result of human efforts. It is God-driven, and for every believer that is persecuted and/or killed there will be countless others coming forward in their stead.

It is a new, surprising time. Because media reporters who have been trained to look for surface news do not always have the ability to see spiritual depth, we should not be surprised that much of what the Christian world sees has been ignored by media. Who knows, it might even be that God designed the ideological tsunami to go unnoticed for a time. But all that is about to be changed. The resistance and even persecution of Christians has increased dramatically, particularly over the last decade, so clearly someone is noticing!

How, you might wonder, can I make these claims? Because it has been foretold: I have simply attempted to take the study of the Scriptures seriously and watch the world the last fifty years. Having said that, no one can tell exactly when all of this will happen. It would be arrogant to try to date the future. This book is not about blood moons or harbingers. It is an attempt to survey what God has clearly promised and compare this to what goes on in the world today in order to infuse you with hope as you face the pressure.

The stage is being set for something dramatic to happen. As the tsunami approaches, don't put on your seat belt and play it safe. This is a time for boldness, endurance, understanding and faith!

Chapter 1

Premise 1: God—We Can Know that He is Here

In this chapter I aim to show that:

1. Belief in God is a moral, not intellectual issue
2. God must, per definition be good
3. God has not hidden Himself—He is revealing His presence so clearly that it is beyond doubt
4. Man does not seek God, so God will seek man
5. Faith can be placed in a fact or a relationship; for instance, 'I believe that the Earth is round' but it can also mean to have faith in a person: trust in God or a neighbor

MY OWN BEGINNING

I grew up in one of the most secular cultures in the world, but I was, of course, not aware of that at the time. Despite this, I became a Christian when I was seven years old. I was on my own in my bedroom as it was past my bedtime. Before I went to sleep I asked God to make me a Christian. He did. I jumped out of bed, went downstairs and shared my newly found faith with everybody

God and the Spiritual Tsunami

in my family. Their reaction was less than enthusiastic. I was reminded, in no uncertain terms, that it was bed time, so back to bed I went. It was not the glorious start of the Christian life that many others describe, but despite this humble beginning, I never forgot my prayer and I never needed to say it again.

None of my close friends were believers, but they were very nice guys. We had a lot of fun, spending every week-end out in the amazing Nordic forests, discussing every part of life that we were aware of. In my experience, nothing (besides knowing God and our family relationships) can be compared to spending midsummer nights in the forest—encountering moose, fox, all kinds of birds and armed only with cameras and fishing gear. Those experiences shaped us all, and to this day I, for one, feel that unless I sleep outside under a bare sky at least once a year, it's a lost year.

Growing up, I realized there was one significant idea that almost everyone seemed to take for granted: one cannot be sure that there is a God, and, if there is a God He is far away, and too busy running the universe to be interested in a cosmically insignificant me. Most religious people who had adopted this mindset seemed really to only expect psychological comfort from their faith, more than tangible reality. So most of my life I was told that I could never be absolutely certain that God exists. To believe in God's existence was purely a matter of blind faith. This ingrained cultural falsehood has profound implications in today's world.

Most people saw faith not as faith in God as He has revealed Himself in the Bible and throughout history, but rather faith in a religious system whose values made the world a better place. Adhering to the values was the only acceptable (albeit a very narrow) definition of faith. Faith, understood as trusting in a personal God that you with intellectual certainty know is there, sounded to many like a contradiction. It was not even on the radar of most people's horizons. Relational faith had been wiped out by years of muddled intellectual work at theological faculties. This uncertainty spread to the largest denominations and from there on to the general population throughout Europe and America. I vividly remember one of my favorite teachers tellingly correcting a friend of mine

Premise 1: God—We Can Know that He is Here

who tried to guess the right answer in geography class: "You may believe when you are in church. In class, we're only interested in facts."

People seemed to think that if God existed He must have withdrawn, and may not really want to be found. My favorite author when I was young, Per Lagerkvist, the Nobel laureate, who had an uncanny ability to speak right into me and many in my generation, worked from that assumption.

I was engrossed in his stories, absorbing some of Lagerkvist's feelings, while not wholly convinced by his world view which seemed to communicate that if there was a God, he was far away, mysterious and unpredictable. While I would never have gone that far, as most teenagers do, I often felt that as humans we were on a lonely and senseless cosmic trip going nowhere. But this hopeless scenario was often overridden by a stirring conviction that there must be more to reality than this.

Lagerkvist grew up in a believing, pietistic home. That particular Christian context was characterized by deep faith, while in its Scandinavian context, it could also be legalistic and a-rational. Within this context, the way to find God was through spiritual and often emotional experiences, and once you had these there was no need for further thought.

Lagerkvist, as well as thousands of others with him, felt alienated by this approach. I suspect Lagerkvist was actually a reluctant rejector of faith in Christ, but it probably seemed to him that existential emptiness and anxiety was the only honest alternative to faith within this scenario. In this way, he became the Existentialist spokesperson for a whole generation of Scandinavians.

The pietistic revivals in the seventeen and eighteen-hundreds swept powerfully over northern Europe and filled the intense longing for God that had been left unanswered by the state churches, but the revivals did not lay a foundation for the continued, healthy growth of the whole church. The consequences of that particular combination—on one hand, a church that was seen as primarily a protector of existing culture and on the other, a renewal movement that was not at all interested in answering the fundamental and honest questions it raised—created, if not the perfect storm, at least the perfect recipe for spiritual apathy.

After a few generations, many now felt that there was no church that seemed interested in giving credible answers, showing the power reality of the early church or with a vision, like the early missionary movements, that brought Christianity to Europe. So the Christian faith came to be looked upon as a crutch for weak people, and secularization logically became a way to prove one's freedom from the spiritually irrelevant ideas of cultural preservation and the religious oppression of legalism.

That was a part of my cultural heritage. I still love and have a deep respect for the revivalist believers I grew up under. Without them—their example, intercession and love—I would probably not be a believer today, and it is out of respect for them that I try to share why it is not only possible, but absolutely necessary, to believe in God.

At the same time, I also have respect for the type of agnosticism and respectful atheism that I have lived alongside all of my life. I don't mean the arrogant and irrational atheism we find in today's best-selling authors trying to dispute the existence of God: authors who come across more like high school bullies than the sensitive analytical minds of men like Lagerkvist or Jürgen Habermas who asked decent and honest questions and who dared to deal with the existential consequences of a life without God. I have met many, thoughtful, but often frustrated persons who are sorely disappointed with religious language without substance and who like one famous philosopher quipped: "Why should I believe in what the church says, when the theologians themselves don't believe it?" I have had the same question myself, so I can appreciate their position. But I have come to see that there are other and better answers—not new answers, by any stretch of the imagination, but old, ageless and clear answers beyond doubt.

Scandinavia is not the only place we find this disillusionment. All across the Western world we find similar issues. While there are many and complex reasons that led to decades of empty, substance-less religiosity, it is a fact that the last two generations have not encountered Christ in a meaningful way. These are the people who now rule the media world and the political machinery. Their pay-check depends on how well they defend the values and lifestyle of their constituency: a constituency that has no idea of who God is and that would rebel against any concept of a supreme Someone who has the final say over their actions. We get a form of closed loop, where everyone reinforces the message and beliefs and becomes more entrenched.

FAITH AND PERSONAL RESPONSIBILITY

But before we look at those old, ageless answers, there is one more aspect that we need to bring up: personal responsibility. You are not destined to become an agnostic or atheist because of the direction taken by your own culture. However little we know, it is our personal responsibility to seek God, and through that relationship with Him to seek to be a blessing to others. That it would be our responsibility might sound like a contradiction to the Western mind, but not in the Semitic worldview—Biblical thinking's original context. The influence of spiritual leaders, cultural direction, personal choices and our response to God's active work in our hearts, are all a part of what makes up the human spiritual journey. Even if all those elements point in conflicting directions, God has left enough revelation around to help us find Him. No one is excused from personal responsibility.

THE FOLLY OF DODGING SCIENCE ARTFULLY

It is neither the will of the majority nor trends in society that decide what is truth, even if the pressure to think like society around us comes from both pundits of the political right and left. The idea of truth is highly controversial today. We cannot live with it, but neither can we live without it. The Bible anchors truth beyond us. It is not found in the majority will of the people or in those who shout the loudest. To extract ourselves from this quagmire we must begin by asking the right questions as honestly and openly as we can. As I have wrestled with the Christian faith as presented in the Bible, I have personally asked a couple of simple questions.

One of the most challenging statements in the Bible is this: "The fool says in his heart, 'There is no God.'" How can the Bible say that, if it is so hard to know that God is here? How can God hold people responsible for not believing what they cannot know for certain?

Assuming that the Bible's assertion here is correct, could it be that, in the West, we have actually unlearned the knowledge of the obvious? That we even suppress the thought of the obvious, like the Bible says we do—a form of what present-day psychologists might describe as perceptual defense? Could it be that even the first verses in the Bible tell us something so obvious that we would kick ourselves for not seeing it earlier?

The beginning is often the best place to start. The first words in the Bible are:

"In the beginning, God created the heavens and the earth." That might sound simple, or even simplistic, but it is the most important piece of concrete information that we have ever given about who He is and who we are.

The first verse in the Bible tells us that there was a beginning of everything in the entire Cosmos. From subatomic particles and galaxies to you and me, we all have our roots in this beginning that happened a long time ago, and this has consequences for us.

If the entire universe had a beginning (a widely accepted scientific view) there must have been a state where there was nothing. No matter, no space, no time, no potentiality. Nothing. Most of us can't imagine that, so we think of nothing as a vast empty space, but there was no space because there would have been no boundaries for that space. Instead, there literally was nothing. Zero.

If we refuse to consider God as the Creator, we are forced to suggest other alternatives to where matter arose from, generating a number of theories about how the universe began out of nothing. These theories are in fact based on the assumption that the universe began out of something, but they cannot explain what

Premise 1: God—We Can Know that He is Here

that 'something' is. All those alternative theories have one thing in common—they are based on a particular leap of faith, i.e. the ill-founded assumption that there is no God. It is certainly possible to suggest other alternatives to God, all of which work on a 'what if' assumption. However, I would maintain that those assumptions are not based on scientific evidence, but are motivated by the common cultural pressure to avoid the God-issue.

Let me illustrate this by taking the idea of the "Big Bang" as the beginning of the universe. Until the early nineteen-hundreds, most physicists believed that the universe was an eternal entity that was renewed because new hydrogen atoms were being made all the time. Because it was discovered that the universe is expanding, a Belgian priest and astronomer, Georges Lemaître suggested that it actually must have had a beginning as a single point billions of years ago. A lot of colleagues criticized the idea, now prevalent, because Lemaître was a Christian and the idea of a beginning of the universe sounded too much like the Genesis creation. The very words "Big Bang" was coined by a British astronomer, Fred Hoyle, who believed in a static universe and who thought the concept of a beginning as in a "Big Bang" was ludicrous. (There was no bang in the beginning, by the way, as there would not have been space enough for sound waves).

Scientific research is a God-given ability and is a deeply Christian pursuit, but the discoveries scientists make do not always sit comfortably with us.

A few years after "Big Bang" was coined, a Russian atheist astronomer, George Gamov, began to underwrite the concept of a beginning of the universe, but as late as the 1950s a number of communist philosophers, who based their ideas on Engels' worldview, asserted that the universe was infinite, eternal, and that the signs of expansion must be explained by other mechanisms. Their most fascinating, anti-scientific argument was that cosmological theories ought to be judged by their correspondence to the dialectical-materialist philosophy. In other words, the current philosophical framework should be the measuring rod by which we interpret scientific discoveries. This was of course the opposite of keeping an open mind. So why would they unapologetically allow personal bias to influence the results? I can only surmise: otherwise we might be led to believe in God.

The question of how matter arose out of nothing is where science becomes personally challenging.

If the only rational explanation for why we are here as human beings is that God has created us, we can infer some basic truths about him.

First, He must be eternal because He was before time. He always was and always will be. God is not made up of matter but is pure spirit—by that I understand He is above matter, space and time. He is the cause of everything that is a part of the space-time creation.

Second, He must be almighty, because He created everything and is the One that makes the whole cosmos work and hold together. How He created and how He holds everything together is beyond what we understand today. As in the case of not being able to grasp nothingness, the very concept of someone being Almighty is also beyond what we understand, but we can understand the rational connection of someone being the Creator of cosmos and that Someone, as a consequence, being almighty. To say that God is almighty is not a 'faith' statement. It is logically necessary to draw that conclusion. Faith, in the light of this, means that we trust in what He has revealed about Himself and in the promises He has given us. When we say that we believe that there is a God and that He is almighty we believe in and accept the logically obvious.

Third, He must be all-knowing, because He is unlimited by space and time. When someone watches what happens on earth, outside of time, both the past and the future is viewable, and for God all this is seen at an instant. There are good reasons to believe that the smallest particles of every atom in the entire universe are actualized because of His awareness of them. So, when Jesus said that not even a single sparrow dies without the Father being aware of it, that was an understatement and should be apparent to anyone who has stopped to reflect on God's omniscience. Since God, according to the Biblical understanding of who He is, holds the

Premise 1: God—We Can Know that He is Here

whole universe together with His Word, He is aware of the most minute detail—be that subatomic particles, sparrows, people or history.

Fourth, He must be what we call omnipresent, because he is above space and time. Space and time relate to what makes up the created universe, and to this day we don't fully understand what they are, although we certainly live under these conditions. To God, the Eternal, who is before the universe that He created, time and space cannot be a limitation for Him. How He chooses to manifest His presence at any place or in any moment is also beyond our understanding, but even in this case His omnipresence must be taken as logically self-evident.

Fifth, since God is the Creator and Sustainer of everything in Cosmos, it follows that He Himself has no needs; rather, He is the Source. He does not need our services, temples, money or anything that we as human beings might need to survive or feel secure. All human attempts to offer sacrifices or services for the sustenance of a perceived god stems from the perception of that 'god' as merely a larger version of ourselves. But that is not the God of the Bible. Since God has no needs, He has created us out of love and is the one who sustains us, not the opposite. The Bible teaches us that God does everything out of love. That He is good. It is His love that motivates His hate of sin, since sin destroys what He has created out of love. It is in this light that we begin to understand how important salvation as a free gift is, and that it is received by grace and faith. Teaching legalistic religion, based on rules of behavior, as a way to find God is an affront to the very essence of who God is. The apostle Paul discusses this in Acts 17:22f.

There follows a surprising consequence of this fact: rejecting God means that you reject the absolute good. If goodness and love is God's essence, then rejecting Him is not rejecting, as we might be tempted to believe, a dictator in order to gain our freedom. Since God is good, rejecting Him is the most fundamental moral evil. It will lead, per definition, to destructive ends for the person that cuts themselves off from the Source of love and goodness, as well as for those who are under the influence of that person or that person's context.

All this means not only that we know that there is a God, but that He must know who you are.

The Bible says that "the fool says in his heart—there is no God." No kidding. We shouldn't believe in God because we are told to, but because there is no other possible way of understanding why there is a world. The person who made that statement knew what many in our part of the world have forgotten or resist. Authors of the various books of the Bible had little patience with bad and irrational thinking and we would do well to follow their example and be encouraged to think for ourselves, and take the necessary steps of reason and be bold enough to dare to believe in God.

My hope is that through the words on the pages of this book you would learn to know more about who God is, how you can get to know His character and to know Him personally—because God reveals Himself clearly to all who want to look at what He does and listen to what He says. He does not try to hide Himself, and the Christian faith is not a blind faith. It is faith in the God who has spoken, who speaks and who invites us to live in fellowship with Him, now and forever.

In light of this vast potential, it is essential that we make sure we're not held back by what others think we should be allowed to think. In a perfect world, it might be wise to thoughtfully follow the wisdom of the majority, but that does not work in a fallen world, where mankind chooses to live in rebellion to God. Freedom to choose does not mean the right to believe anything, regardless of the consequences. It does mean that I am free (and not held back) to believe what I know is right, regardless of what anyone else thinks I ought to believe.

Chapter 1b . . . .

Follow-up: A Look at Paul's Letter to the Romans

The Bible tells us that we have an innate knowledge of God. Paul, a convert himself a few years after Jesus' death, describes how chaos follows in the wake of the denial and rejection of God.

Chapter one of the Letter to the Romans in the New Testament is one of the most criticized parts of the Bible, partly because of what it says and partly for what it is perceived to say. One thing is certain, however: Paul, like his co-writers in the Bible, argues that the knowledge of God is so obviously clear that there is no excuse for not believing and trusting in God.

THIS IS HOW PAUL'S ARGUMENT GOES

In verse 16 Paul affirms that he is not ashamed of the message that God has given us. Think about this: if you are a leading representative of a persecuted movement, and as one of its leaders you are more persecuted than others, that might be a valid reason to feel like an underdog in society and lead to a sense of inferiority. But (unless you have serious mental health issues) if you are absolutely certain that what you represent is true, and that in the end it will be made clear to all that you were right all along, then there is no reason to feel belittled. Paul was like that. The Gospel is not only theoretical truth—it has the power to change lives now and forever. It is a message, but it is also power. It does not only carry power, it is power! As God created the cosmos by His word, so the proclamation of the Gospel causes the changes that it describes.

For those who receive the message by faith it provides divine righteousness (verse 17). Righteousness has legal overtones and means 'being made right' or 'being blameless'. Despite all the ways we have disregarded our Creator and played God ourselves, trampled on His creation and gone our own way to the detriment of ourselves and those around us, God 'justifies' those who accept the news of His rescue wholeheartedly. That tells us about God's love. This radical, definite righteousness is not earned, but is a free gift. Neither does God put unreasonable demands on people to make them feel worthless, useless and alienated from hope. Instead, He provides for the basic need that enables men to live in fellowship with Himself again—the absolute Holy One—a perfect righteousness that is granted as a gift for those who receive it by simple faith. When we look at the life of Jesus in the Gospels it is made clear, beyond any possible misunderstanding, that God has no problem with receiving repentant sinners, but thoroughly seems to dislike self-righteousness.

This is the background to Paul's description of the wrath of God over sin. As we see in this context, sin is fundamentally the result of rejecting God, and not primarily an issue of wrong behavior. The rejection of God comes first; the behavior follows. This was not only a radical message to many in the early Church who fought for non-Jewish believers to be subjected to the Old Testament law and regulations. It is also a radical message to many twenty-first century Christians who spend extreme amounts of energy forcing Christian life-styles on secular people through the political system and thereby alienating them from the very Church that is called to lead them to faith in Jesus Christ through repentance. Putting the cart before the horse is an age-long temptation and is almost always based on bad theology.

God, we learn, is most certainly angry over sin. His wrath over sin is constantly being revealed in a surprising way: God allows people to follow their desires for instant self-gratification and to experience the ultimate consequences of these desires. But since God has left them to do what they want, they are not even aware of His absence and think they have reached the heights of independence. This is the ultimate self-delusion and results in chaos. It is not possible to persuade people who have gone this far to repentance and faith. As Paul shows us later in the book of Romans, only an act of God Himself can save them now.

PAUL EXPOSES THE ROAD TO CULTURAL CHAOS

The chaos begins with a denial of the clearly perceived reality of God. Creation is a powerful witness to God. He is the originator of all creation, which among other things means that He was before anything was created. He is eternal and has power that exceeds our understanding. He is the definition of Divine. The proper response to knowing that He has made us, in whatever way He did, is to honor, trust and thank Him. For past believers, this has led to an understanding that God is inherently holy, good and loving.

The most sobering and helpful insight we could ever have is, "There is a God, and it is not me." Our response must logically be to listen to what He tells us as He is the reason why we exist, to trust Him and then do what He tells us to do.

When humanity decides to be the master of its own destiny it will by necessity end in disaster. We will look into why this is in the next chapter, but if you disagree, it's helpful to watch the evening news, any day of the week. We live in a time when many worry that mankind is about to saw off the branch it's sitting on, but still we irrationally put our hope in the secular sages who tell us that they, or someone they have heard of, has the solution to the human mire of war, ethnic cleansing, refugees & slavery, financial disasters, violence & terror, environmental problems, incurable disease and a hundred percent mortality rate. We allow ourselves to be convinced and we put our trust in virtually anyone who sounds like they have the answer, even when the person has a proven track record of insincerity and corruption.

The understanding of how the world operates explains why the next phrase follows: ". . .The wrath of God is revealed against all ungodliness and unrighteousness of men. . ." One surprising aspect of this is that we should not expect the wrath of God to only be released in the future, even though that will happen, but the Apostle tells us that it is happening right now, in a very dramatic way: God leaves rebels to do what they want to for the time being. Quite a sobering thought.

And this is not unfair. In verse 19 Paul reminds us that what can be known about God through pure reason is obvious, since creation itself witnesses loud and clear to the reality of His eternal power.

He goes so far as to remind us that once all humanity knew the truth about God. He says that the truth is still discoverable. In fact, the question of knowing whether God exists or not does not lie with the secular evidence, or lack of it, but with the human heart. Humanity is rejecting the knowledge of God and is actively suppressing it, and refuses to honor and be thankful—rejecting the source of all goodness because of the perception that independence from God is the greatest freedom or the most glorious expression of our humanity.

Living in this enormously beautiful and complex world without access to the wisdom of its Creator can only lead to disintegration. We do not have the knowledge and wisdom needed. We might impress someone with our knowledge of significant amounts of detail about the world, but that's only possible as long as those we impress are not aware of the vastness of and unfathomable variety in the universe and the complexity even on this tiny, but fantastic planet that we live on. Just read a doctoral dissertation and you'll see, that although it is impressive to most of us, the candidate hasn't actually mastered more than a tiny detail from their field. From this perspective it is clear that denying our need for God is pure arrogance.

All of the sins that are listed in this text in Romans 1, and it is a most unpopular list, flow out of this fundamental rejection of God. It is also crystal clear from the text that one cannot live with these behaviors, and also, at the same time, claim to believe in God. Because faith in God is far more than believing in His existence. As we have seen, it is allowing His existence and the knowledge of who He is to influence how we live our lives.

So, in summary, the Apostle's reasoning leads us to the conclusion that belief in God is not primarily a rational issue. It turns out to be a moral issue: one either accepts the facts or knowingly suppress them, with whatever consequences that follow.

Finally, there is one more surprising twist in the text. It looks like this: men choose to rebel against God, so God judges them, i.e. leaves them to follow their own desires, to follow false gods and lead destructive lifestyles. This judgment is so severe that they no longer even understand how foolish their choices are. And then here comes the twist: despite this, God does not abandon us. Jesus Christ came to save us from the well-earned wrath of God. This good news, the Gospel, is the one thing that can change us. It is the message about who Jesus Christ is and what He did for us, and how He introduces the new reality of God's present salvation for us and the invitation to live with Him instead of without Him. But it is more than a message, it is God's power of salvation—it is the one thing that can open the hearts and minds of a rebellious humanity to the new reality of Jesus as Lord and Savior.

Here is the text in full from Paul's Epistle to the Romans, chapter 1, verses 16—32. Notice the flow of the argument: the Gospel is the power of God for salvation, and rejecting God and His invitation to salvation will lead to severe problems and the final separation from God that those who reject that Gospel are themselves choosing at this present time.

16 For I am not ashamed of the gospel, for it is the power of God for salvation to everyone who believes, to the Jew first and also to the Greek. 17 For in it the righteousness of God is revealed from faith for faith, as it is written, "The righteous shall live by faith." 18 For the wrath of God is revealed from heaven against all

ungodliness and unrighteousness of men, who by their unrighteousness suppress the truth. 19 For what can be known about God is plain to them, because God has shown it to them. 20 For his invisible attributes, namely, his eternal power and divine nature, have been clearly perceived, ever since the creation of the world, in the things that have been made. So they are without excuse. 21 For although they knew God, they did not honor him as God or give thanks to him, but they became futile in their thinking, and their foolish hearts were darkened. 22 Claiming to be wise, they became fools, 23 and exchanged the glory of the immortal God for images resembling mortal man and birds and animals and creeping things. 24 Therefore God gave them up in the lusts of their hearts to impurity, to the dishonoring of their bodies among themselves, 25 because they exchanged the truth about God for a lie and worshiped and served the creature rather than the Creator, who is blessed forever! Amen. 26 For this reason God gave them up to dishonorable passions. For their women exchanged natural relations for those that are contrary to nature; 27 and the men likewise gave up natural relations with women and were consumed with passion for one another, men committing shameless acts with men and receiving in themselves the due penalty for their error. 28 And since they did not see fit to acknowledge God, God gave them up to a debased mind to do what ought not to be done. 29 They were filled with all manner of unrighteousness, evil, covetousness, malice. They are full of envy, murder, strife, deceit, maliciousness. They are gossips, 30 slanderers, haters of God, insolent, haughty, boastful, inventors of evil, disobedient to parents, 31 foolish, faithless, heartless, ruthless. Though they know God's righteous decree that those who practice such things deserve to die, they not only do them but give approval to those who practice them.

This is not the end of the story. After looking into the problem of sin, in the next chapter, we will in see in the rest of the book that God actively seeks man. He reveals Himself clearly, makes promises to those who dare to believe Him and He fulfills those promises even over very long time periods.

Chapter 2

Premise 2: Sin is Our Problem but God Does Not Leave Us

In this chapter I aim to show that:

1. God is not the reason for chaos in the world
2. Man was created to lead what happens on the Earth, but in relation and in cooperation with God
3. It is possible to be a blessing even in a fallen world
4. There is a way to relate to God again, but it must be on God's terms

MY DILEMMA

Over the years I discovered I wasn't the only one who wrestled personally with the question of what sin really is. A common, underlying idea in the world about sin seems to go something like this: God created a world that was rigged from the beginning to the disadvantage of man. He then set up rules for living that are impossible to live up to and He checks up on us all the time to see if we follow His rules. God is seen as a cosmic super-police. A common unspoken misconception is therefore that we as humans are the victims and God is the culprit. You are not going to hear any believing Christians say that out loud, but it is often communicated indirectly.

A related issue is what happens to people who have never heard the Christian Gospel. Can they come to heaven anyway, or are they condemned because they never had the opportunity to meet a Christian who would tell them? Why couldn't God be fair, just forgive them and take them to heaven? For centuries, some Christians have argued this way and tried to find some loophole to solve the emotional dilemma they created for themselves.

The question becomes especially hard when a non-Christian friend, a good person from a human standard, asks: "So you think I will go to hell just because I don't believe in God the way you do?" Now, suddenly it is not only God who seems unfair, but I also, who apparently am colluding with Him on this. I have found myself in this uncomfortable situation a number of times.

But getting into uncomfortable situations can be a good thing, if it forces us to think: What is it that I am saying, and what do I really believe? Many good books have been written on the subject of sin. Some well-known authors are Augustine of Hippo, Martin Luther and one of my favorites, John Owen. But there is usually more to a story than meets the eye. As is often the case in the Bible and its Semitic world-view, a thing can be true while not ruling out another aspect needed for a fuller understanding. I am not saying truth is relative, but Truth in the Bible is often revealed in a way that those who come from a Western culture haven't been trained to follow.

The Biblical world-view does not shy away from complexity the way the West is inclined to do. In order to understand Biblical revelation, we need to keep two or three factors alive at the same time and balance these as a juggler would. The juggler has the challenging task of keeping several balls in the air at once. Doing a similar trick with ideas is even more stretching, but in the case of what the Bible shows, it is necessary and helps us stay closer to reality. The story about Adam and Even in the Garden of Eden is such a case.

Premise 2: Sin is Our Problem but God Does Not Leave Us

THE GARDEN OF EDEN

The story about Adam and Eve in the Garden of Eden introduces a deeper understanding of what sin is. The story is saturated with historic information and symbolism, and is transmitted in a cultural language that has made it difficult for Westerners to intuitively understand it. Since it is hard to grasp with Western eyes, it is tempting to interpret the story as mythological, akin to other Near Eastern folklore. We tend to use that approach with the Eden-story but in doing so we often fail to hear its message about the basic reason for the human dilemma.

Genesis 1 tells us that God is the Creator of everything there is. He is the Originator of the space-time cosmos. We also learn that He is the Originator of the rich and enormously complex biological variation on the earth, where He put man to be His representative. Just the study of basic biology is baffling: how complex, intricate and interdependent the different species are and how even an individual cell is an elaborate enterprise. And to scientists' recent astonishment they are becoming aware how the whole earth should be seen as one supra complex interdependent system. The earth in its entirety is actually the most highly organized and information dense cosmic body we are aware of in the universe.

God put man on this unique planet, and man was created in the image of God. As in much Semitic literature, a word can have a variety of meanings. So it is with the concept of man being created in the image of God. Amongst images of similarity of image or character, or thoughts of sentient ability or creativity, the term also conveys the sense of man being God's representative, or vice-ruler.[1]

---

1. There is good scholarly material available to anyone who would like to study more about the background of why we can claim that this is one of the ideas underlying the story of Eden. One example is J. Richard Middleton, who is close to Martin Luther's view that the image of God was really meant to convey Adam's and Eve's call to rule the earth. Many others, like St. Augustine of Hippo have written extensively on other aspects of the "image," so in this chapter, we will focus on the "image of God" with reference to man's call to represent God as vice-ruler.

God and the Spiritual Tsunami

MAN AS GOD'S VICE-REGENT ON EARTH

If we read the story about the creation and Eden carefully, it quickly becomes rather obvious that there is more to the Garden of Eden than we see from just a casual reading. The Garden had a gate that later needed to be guarded. There were cherubim, who only appear in the Bible in relation to the Garden of Eden, the Temple in Jerusalem and the presence of God in heaven. Eden was the place where God most clearly revealed His presence. It was faced toward the east, as the Temple would be, and a river flowed out of it that was later divided into four heads, which reminds us about Ezekiel's prophecy of a new Temple with a river flowing out from it. The concept of Eden as a Temple looks rather convincing, and is mentioned/discussed in both the Talmud and Midrash.[2]

The Temple is a place where humans commune with and receive guidance from God. Adam and Eve were created in the image of God, put in this Temple-Garden, Eden, and their task was to take care of the earth. From Eden they were to bring God's order and blessing to the rest of the world.

26 Then God said, "Let us make man in our image, after our likeness. And let them have dominion over the fish of the sea and over the birds of the heavens and over the livestock and over all the earth and over every creeping thing that creeps on the earth."

27 So God created man in his own image, in the image of God he created him; male and female he created them.

28 And God blessed them. And God said to them, "Be fruitful and multiply and fill the earth and subdue it, and have dominion over the fish of the sea and over the birds of the heavens and over every living thing that moves on the earth." Genesis 1:26–28.

Humankind, man and woman, was given responsibility by God to take care of the Garden of Eden and the whole earth: to, in effect, be God's vice-regents. As a matter of fact, this task is central to our purpose—and the responsibility is something every human carries with them. We can liken this to a person who has become

---

2. Jewish Rabbinic texts commenting on and interpreting the Old Testament.

Premise 2: Sin is Our Problem but God Does Not Leave Us

a parent—the fact that someone has become a parent cannot be undone. He or she can be a good parent, a bad parent or an absent parent, but the fact of being a parent, the influence for good or bad and the responsibility that is attached, never goes away. In the same way, the call and responsibility to be vice-regents endures. It was meant to be carried out in communion with God and according to His perfect will.

The crucial point to remember is this: since man is a vice-regent, he is obviously meant to be under the leadership of the Ultimate Ruler—God, the Creator. In other words, humanity was created to take care of Eden and the earth, to be the agent who, step by step, was meant to bring about God's blessing and order to the entire planet.

When God told Adam to name all the animals, Adam would be taking the first step to exercise that authority. Naming each species in creation was more than an intellectual action; it was accepting the responsibility given, demonstrating authority and taking the first step to rule under God.

God's purpose for creating man on the earth was to reveal His eternal characteristic to sustain and bless what He had created, and, in turn, for mankind to be a 'conduit' for that blessing. Humans were never intended to use creation for their own self-magnification, by acting like they were gods or using its resources mainly for self-gratification. Man needed the guidance, influence, power and wisdom of God in order to be good vice-regents and to handle the delegated authority responsibly.

We hopefully begin to see how important it is that mankind lives in trusting dependence on God, particularly in light of the supra-complex interaction between matter and biological diversity. No living person has ever been able to understand how all the created order works together. Even after hundreds of years of documented study, scientists continue to observe and discover new phenomena.[3]

---

3. "Mycorrhizal networks," at: https://www.ted.com/talks/suzanne_simard_how_trees_talk_to_each_other/transcript?language=en.

God and the Spiritual Tsunami

When we live independently of God, even with the best intentions, anything we touch or change on earth seems eventually to leads to disastrous consequences, even if that change momentarily looks like a good idea. From plastic[4] and carbon dioxide to nuclear energy, the greatest fear of many today is that mankind is about to destroy the very earth it depends on for its survival. That destructive process began with the first humans acting independently.

There is further Biblical information that adds another important layer to the picture. The Bible shows us that the world is also influenced powerfully by spiritual beings, and that there has been a war against man's commitment to his Maker and his calling since the earliest times. To believe that, we of course need to feel confident that the Bible is presenting an accurate picture of reality; we will look at that in Chapter 3. Until then, presuppose that we do need to take spiritual reality into account when we consider humanity's attempt to run life without God. In this light, humanity's attempt is, quite simply, doomed to fail.

The first humans at first had all they needed to fulfill their calling. They lived in the presence of God and communicated freely with him, similar to the experience of Moses,[5] but did so only in a partial way. Jesus Christ would later fully reveal what that communication was meant to be like.

The first humans knew what to do and what not to do. It was not a full, immediate knowledge (an innate God-consciousness that we just need to get in touch with) that some non-Biblical religions claim they can offer. This would really be the kind of access to information that makes humans independent of a personal God. What God intends for us is a 'knowing', as and when we need it, flowing from a personal fellowship with God. It was meant to be incremental, and would be added to as time and experience allowed.

---

4. "Eight Million Tons of Plastic Dumped in Ocean Every Year," at: http://news.nationalgeographic.com/news/2015/02/150212-ocean-debris-plastic-garbage-patches-science/.

5. Exodus 33:11.

Premise 2: Sin is Our Problem but God Does Not Leave Us

Depending on our own family history, we might be tempted to think of this in terms of dysfunctional family strategies for controlling each other, but this is not the way of God. It was not a way to tie humans to God—this is not how the God of the Bible works. Instead, it freed humans from the burden of needing to know everything for survival. It allows God to be God and humans to be humans.

An example of this incremental sharing is God telling Adam he is free to eat of all the fruit in the garden, except from the tree of the Knowledge of Good and Evil. At that point he was informed of one consequence, the most devastating one, of disobeying that instruction. He was later to discover there were other consequences from his disobedience as well, not of the same magnitude as death, but so serious that it would affect the whole earth he had been set to rule.

Not only did they have access to the knowledge they needed to fulfill their calling; they were also enabled. Because when God speaks, in the Biblical context, He is not just sharing ideas, but His very words are power. God's words and God's acts are one. God did not call them into a difficult or burdensome task, since He would enable them with His power. The difficulties and burdens came as a result of the rebellion, when humans were successfully tempted by the enemy to act independently of God, or, more precisely, humans attempted to become god.[6] Bad idea for so many reasons.

LET GOD BE GOD

As long as humans lived in the kind of relationship with God that they were created for, they were a blessing to the earth. God's goodness and generosity were manifest to them and through what they did. When they left that intimate fellowship, they pulled the earth along with them into the consequences of the curse that followed them and their descendants through the ages.

---

6. Genesis 3:5.

The earth, small though it is from a cosmic perspective, is such a beautiful, complex organism. We, as humans, just do not have the mental capacity for the knowledge needed to influence it in a way that leads to long-term, sustainable development and global harmony. In fact, the Bible tells us to beware of the human who claims to have that coordinating power. Anyone who has ever thought about the idea of super-complex realities understands that it would take superhuman abilities to get it right. And being human is, by definition, not being super-human.

When Adam and Eve revolted against God and decided to try to be gods themselves, one of the results was that the earth would no longer yield its produce in the generous way they were used to, but it would take hard work and they would harvest thorns and thistles with the produce they needed. So much for the claim that religion is just a personal, private matter. The earth, their own children and the whole of mankind suffered the consequences with them.

FAITH, OR LACK OF, IS NEVER A PRIVATE MATTER

It is clear from the Eden story that sin, i.e. the rebellion against God, favoring independence over fellowship, was not just a private matter. It was a personal choice, to be sure, but one that had catastrophic consequences for everything that existed and exists on the earth.

We see that one of the many aspects of sin is that it affects all of us. Adam is responsible for putting us all in the horrible state of what is called original sin, a perpetual disconnection from our Maker and a fallen nature that prefers evil to good. This makes it impossible to live in this fallen world without sinning. Continue to bear in mind that the purpose of man is to serve God, with God's wisdom, instruction and blessing, as well as live in a vital relationship with Him. It is therefore obvious that without this relationship with God, we will bring problems and chaos along with us wherever we settle and live on earth.

Premise 2: Sin is Our Problem but God Does Not Leave Us

All humans are born into this fallen state, and they willingly continue to live apart from God until God takes an initiative to free them to become what they were created to be. But to think that we can outsmart complex chaos by our own cleverness—by introducing better scientific methods and solutions—are signs of ignorance at best and pure arrogance at worst.

Science and technology have, of course, been a blessing in many ways. I believe they were meant to be. But the discoveries made are haphazard, a few pieces only from a huge puzzle, and no human has the bigger picture or the power to coordinate these findings. Without direction, mankind's worst fear of the potential destruction of the planet (that we are bringing on ourselves but blaming others for) looms large.

We are not super-humans, but one thing we do have is influence. God created us to have influence and to rule over the earth. As we saw earlier, we cannot stop having influence any more than a biological parent can stop being a parent once their child is born. We can be a good or bad, a present or absent parent. Even when a child is legally adopted by somebody else, the biological parental influence is still there. Our influence is significant.

JOSEPH AND DANIEL

There are stories that demonstrate how important it is for individuals to live in trusting fellowship with God, even though the world is fallen and dysfunctional. The stories show how a believer in God is meant to be an influence and a blessing to the world. Joseph in the book of Genesis and Daniel, one of the prophets, are good examples. The ultimate illustration is, of course, Jesus Christ himself.

The story of Joseph is an illustration of how one person, in personal relationship with God, becomes a blessing to two nations. Joseph, one of Jacob's children, had been sold as a slave in Egypt by his brothers. What Joseph and his brothers were not aware of in the beginning of this story, was that God was going to turn the brothers' intent for evil into something that He would later use to

God and the Spiritual Tsunami

save their lives, while simultaneously ensuring His solemn promise to Abraham was fulfilled.

Despite Joseph's upbringing in a dysfunctional family, he chose to live for God. He was sold as a slave to Potiphar, one of Pharaoh's officials, and following one invitation after another to go to bed with Potiphar's wife, he still refused and said that he would not sin against God. He never lost the plot: he understood that life is not about instant gratification, but about serving God's greater purposes.

The story goes on and tells us that Potiphar's household was blessed because Joseph was in his house. God was with him. On the back of his refusal to commit adultery, he was falsely accused and sent to prison in disgrace. The reward for his faithfulness was not immediate. In fact, instead of immediate reward there was immediate persecution. But even in that situation God was with Joseph and blessed him.

After years of hardship Joseph ended up as a close adviser to the Egyptian Pharaoh himself. The background was that Pharaoh had a dream that foretold the next fourteen years, but neither Pharaoh, nor his religious advisors could interpret the dream. Joseph was invited to interpret it and then to prepare the country for the predicted famine. There is no known human method, then or now, that can foresee such dramatic yet transient changes years in advance. Only God holds such knowledge. In order to act wisely, Pharaoh appointed Joseph to be in charge of the strategic processes leading up to and through those hard years which, in the most remarkable way, led to the reunification and reconciliation of Joseph's family, and in time led to the birth of Israel as a nation.

A second illustration is the prophet Daniel, who lived almost a millennium later. He and a large group of Jewish leading families had been taken as captives to Babylon. That period, called the Babylonian captivity, came as a punishment from God for the 'second' revolt (after Adam's) when the leading political and religious leaders in Judah chose to go back into idolatry, criminal behavior and immorality. In spite of the influences of the Babylonian powerful foreign culture, Daniel and some of his friends decided to live for

Premise 2: Sin is Our Problem but God Does Not Leave Us

and trust in God to the degree that they put their own lives at risk, rather than abandoning their faith in God.

Daniel, like Joseph, served a powerful, foreign king while sorely criticized and undermined by some of his colleagues. But he was needed to help the nation get through the turbulent times of exile that the elite had brought upon the people. Daniel himself survived a number of empires that came and went during his life in Babylon. He continued to reprove and challenge their kings to live and rule responsibly. His prophetic predictions were so accurate that modernistic theologians, who do not accept the possibility of divine prophecy, tend to dismiss the probability that Daniel authored the book that bears his name.

JESUS AND THE KINGDOM OF GOD

The clearest proclamation of what an enormous blessing one person can be when he fully trusts God came through Jesus Christ. He is so important in the history of what God is doing that the New Testament calls him 'the new Adam', the one who undoes the mess that the first Adam made.

Jesus and the apostles teach without any shadow of a doubt that Jesus Christ is the unique Son of God, and thereby truly God himself. The apostle John wrote in John 1:1–3, referring to Jesus as 'The Word': "In the beginning was the Word, and the Word was with God, and the Word was God. He was in the beginning with God. All things were made through him, and without him was not anything made that was made" (John 1:1–3 ESV). It cannot be stated more clearly than this, can it?

At the same time, Jesus also stated that while He walked on earth, He did not perform miracles by His own power. Having emptied himself at birth of His Divine glory, while on earth He chose to act with only the same power that all humans possess. He waited for the guidance of the Father and made Himself dependent on the power of the Holy Spirit. He said: "Truly, truly, I say to you, the Son can do nothing of his own accord, but only what he sees the Father doing. For whatever the Father does, that the Son does likewise." (John 5:19 ESV) When His opponents questioned His modus operandi, he challenged them by claiming: "But if it is by the finger of God that I cast out demons, then the kingdom of God has come upon you" (Luke 11:20 ESV).

Wherever Jesus walked the sick were healed, dead were raised, storms were subdued as nature responded instantly to His commands. The point here is that Jesus was careful to explain that He did not do these things in His own power, which He easily could have done, being God, but He did them as a true man who was the promised Messiah/Christ and who would rule the earth under the Kingship of God.

The Gospel is said to be about the fact that the Kingdom of God was manifest by His presence. In Mark 1:14–15 we read: "Now after John was arrested, Jesus came into Galilee, proclaiming the gospel of God, and saying, 'The time is fulfilled, and the kingdom of God is at hand; repent and believe in the gospel.'" (ESV). In Jesus' life we see God's intention to bring blessing and wholeness to the earth (His Kingdom), and reveal His goodness, generosity and power for all to see. And one day he will fulfill this plan through all those who have believed Him, as the Apostle Paul reminds us in Ephesians: "To me, though I am the very least of all the saints, this grace was given, to preach to the Gentiles the unsearchable riches of Christ, and to bring to light for everyone what is the plan of the mystery hidden for ages in God who created all things, so that through the church the manifold wisdom of God might now be made known to the rulers and authorities in the heavenly places. This was according to the eternal purpose that he has realized in Christ Jesus our Lord. . ." (Ephesians 3:8–11 ESV)

Jesus Christ did what Adam failed to do—He chose to trust the Father completely and to only do what the Father wanted Him to do at every moment. Despite living in the fallen world and being rejected by the leaders of this world, He changed the course of history. He revealed what it means to live under God's rule, which is called the Kingdom of God, even to the point of death. Through that death and the example of His life He made it possible for others to enter that Kingdom and that extraordinary relationship with God.

THE ESSENCE OF SIN

What we have seen so far is that the most fundamental aspect of sin is rebellion against God and trying to be god on one's own. That rebellion leads to alienation from God and the dysfunction of the created order on earth. Living in that state is called 'sin' both because it is dishonoring to God but also because humans are unable to fulfill the purpose for which they were created—we fall short of our calling. The only solution to the most fundamental of all problems is to accept reality and come back to God on the conditions that God, the Creator and Sustainer Himself, has offered.

Even if we deny it vehemently, when we choose to live life apart from God our unguided ambitions and actions will lead to suffering and chaos. Sin is a far deeper problem and far more complex than most modern/secular persons would admit. It is of course more obvious in some cases than others, because some people seem to 'have it all together'. But God provided a litmus test.

THE LAW AND THE TEN COMMANDMENTS

The purpose of the Old Testament law and the Ten Commandments was partly to help the people of Israel to live in the most favorable environment possible in this dysfunctional, fallen world. But it also fulfills another function. We are told that the law cannot bring salvation from the predicament that mankind finds itself in but it acts as a standard from which we can identify our sin. If someone were able to live fully in harmony with the law they were promised life, but the story of the Old Testament is that no one ever did that. Only Jesus Christ, the Son of God, did that when He was born to live on earth and through His life, death and resurrection brings life to all who receive Him.

God and the Spiritual Tsunami

The ultimate consequence of the law is the revelation that man, in his rebellious state, is both unable and unwilling to do what God wants. When we look at the essence of the Ten Commandments we see that they emphasize faith in God as step one—a willingness to live according to His standards and thus act in the best interest of others. It really is that simple, but not one of us has fully lived that way. The teaching in the New Testament, therefore, shows us that since God is good and generous He uses the law to prepare the world for the arrival of the Savior. He makes the world aware of its sin and introduces none other than God, the Son Himself, who lets Himself be crucified to atone for those sins.

Since sin is different in its essence from what is popularly understood, we begin to see that although acts of sin certainly trespass on God's standard, the root and most grievous sin is that of revolting against a good, generous and holy God and then acting like we ourselves are gods. We do that by either exchanging the true God for gods of our own choosing, which is also called idolatry, and/or by claiming that we ourselves are the highest authority of what is right and moral on earth, which is the more arrogant alternative, called atheism, or its feebler form, agnosticism.

The only way back to God is for man to accept the way He offers to a restored fellowship with Himself. The most witless mistake any human could make would be to try to get back to God on one's own merits. Such an attempt would only illustrate the depth of his arrogance and rebellion. The proof that any person wants to break with humanity's past is to accept the way back that God Himself has provided. Nothing else makes sense.

Chapter 3

Follow the Signs—Israel

In this chapter I aim to show that:

1. God reveals Himself clearly in contemporary history
2. He does what He said He would do in a way that we all can see it
3. God will reveal Himself in Him the way he decides is best
4. God's purpose with revealing Himself has always been to bless
5. God does not tell us everything we would like to know, but He tells us enough so we will be able to commit our lives to Him

HOW GOD REVEALS HIMSELF

The question of God's revelation of Himself begs the question: why doesn't God reveal himself even more clearly, audibly and visibly, announce His existence with a booming voice and a triumphal stage entry, and make us pay attention? Relationship (at the heart of His desire for us) cannot be forced. He leaves signs that speak loud and clear if we're looking (If you seek me with all your heart, you will find me!), but if we do not want to hear, we won't hear; if we don't want to see we won't see. Just as when Jesus came and demonstrated who he was: many still did not believe. We don't see because we do not want to see. Jesus tells the story of the rich man and Lazarus. The rich man (who was in Hell) begged God to send Lazarus (who was in Heaven) to warn His brothers. But Jesus says, "If they did not listen to Moses and the Prophets, they won't listen now . . ."

The key is wholeheartedness. Wholeheartedness is the key to every warm and sincere relationship. This is what God gives us—His heart and His absolute sincerity. But it's also what He desires in return.

The literary hero of my youth, Per Lagerkvist, was wrong in his basic existential assumptions. God does not hide Himself. On the contrary, He reveals Himself so clearly that it easily blinds, offends and shocks us. He was there to be seen during Lagerkvist's time just like He is now.

God does not only want us to believe He exists, but, far more importantly, He wants us to know and trust Him. God's revelation of Himself is designed to enable us to learn things about His character—that He is trustworthy and good.

You might wonder how we can know anything about God's character apart from what we read in the Bible. For starters, take a look at the historical arguments for why the Christian faith is true. The historicity of Jesus' resurrection, the beginning of the Church and fulfilled Biblical prophecies are some of them. One who looked at those arguments was the late, former atheist philosopher, Anthony Flew. He wrote that over time he came to see the arguments for Jesus' resurrection as much stronger than he had previously understood. He ended up writing a book called "There Is a God."

Not only are there the historical arguments, but there are also things happening right before our eyes that verify the truth about the Biblical records. Look at what is happening around the people of Israel, the growth of the Church and the present persecution of the Church: it's all there. We will look into all that.

Follow the Signs—Israel

No other generation in the history of mankind has had such clear reminders as ours has had of how God acts in history to fulfill his purposes—how He is always faithful to what He has said. Whether we like what we see or not, from a Biblical perspective, it is a remarkable time to be alive.

GOD REVEALS HIMSELF IN THE WAY HE THINKS IS BEST

If God were to reveal Himself and His purposes, He would probably do it in a way that was clear and evident, but He would, of course, do it in His own way. Therefore, we should not ask questions about Him that fit only one particular time, ethnic, cultural or religious group, which is the anthropocentric (man-centered) approach. The only intellectually honest approach I can think of is to aim to step out of my own shoes and ask: if God really has revealed Himself (beyond the fundamentals we glean from thinking about the creation of cosmos) how might He do that and what consequences can we draw from what we have learned about Him?

This is a simple but surprisingly radical approach that should turn some epistemological systems upside down and might lead us to embrace realities that would be challenging for many—if it indeed is true that the world lives in rebellion to God.

Well, is it? I always find it helps to consider our own place in the universe. If the size of the universe really is more than 13 billion light-years, if it contains at least 200 billion galaxies (and may be many, many more) that each contain on average at least 200 billion stars, and our planet circles one of its medium sized stars, it would be an understatement to claim that this would make humans on earth statistically insignificant. That would be the case if size and cosmological statistics were the main standard.

If the God who created all this chose to speak to us, infinitesimal as we are, He would most certainly feel free to do that on His own terms while expecting the receivers of His revelation to listen attentively and humbly. Surely this would not be too much to expect? But because of our rebellion against Him and our flawed perspective, the human response is a mixed bag. We confuse size and value and fail to recognize greatness when we see it.

Consider this: Jesus, aka the Creator of the world, was born in one of the smallest cities in a small Roman province, under God's precise direction. Jesus was sentenced not by the Emperor of Rome, but by a minor governor in that small Roman province and He was resurrected in the capital of that province, Jerusalem. If the Roman Emperor had heard of it, and he probably didn't, he would not have taken it very seriously. But looking at those events from a cosmic perspective, we see that they were fundamental and decisive, reversing the laws of death and changing history. They also encourage a radical departure from traditional ways of evaluating the importance of events. This is exactly the kind of background we need to begin to see the significance of God's revelation to Abraham, and what we can see of its consequences right before our eyes today.

So we see how God's revelation of Himself is designed to enable us to learn things about His character—that He is trustworthy and good. But He also intends and desires for us to begin to know Him personally and to have a person to person relationship with Him based on trust. However, the only way to build that relationship is by practicing trusting obedience and learning how absolutely true He is to what He has promised.

It is abundantly clear in the Bible that God can only be truly known as people hear His call and follow Him by faith. This is because God has chosen to reveal himself as a person who can only be known in a personal way. Simply knowing the fact that God exists as an eternal, all-powerful and all-knowing Being is not the same as knowing God the way He designed us to know Him. James, the leader of the first church in Jerusalem and the author of the Epistle of James wrote in James 2:19: "You believe that God is one; you do well. Even the demons believe-and shudder!" The devil and the demons are aware of the existence of God, but this knowledge does them no good. It is as we show our faith in active obedience that we begin to understand truths about God, and it is also the way we show others what Biblical faith is about.

Just as creation reveals the power and glory of God, so do God's acts in history in partnership with the faith of believers. These together reveal His love, power and faithfulness and the reality of Biblical faith.

A look into some aspects of Abraham's life will hopefully make these abstract claims more concrete. Observing his life will help us to see how Abraham got to know God, how it affected his life, the history of his descendants and how it makes the truth about God's existence and rule over the history on earth known to everyone to this very day.

HOW ABRAHAM GOT TO KNOW GOD

Abraham's first steps of faith.

Abraham was born in the city of Ur into a culture of idolatry. It was one of the highest developed cultures of its time, but had drifted away from the spiritual roots that were based on what God had said and done in history. By letting that happen, Ur unwittingly succumbed to spiritual decadence that lead to its ultimate destruction.

In Joshua 24:2 we are told that God called Abraham to leave that destructive culture and to follow Him. Joshua told the story to the people by starting it this way, "This is what the Lord, the God of Israel, says: 'Long ago your ancestors, including Terah the father of Abraham and Nahor, lived beyond the Euphrates River and worshiped other gods. . .'"

THE FIRST IMPORTANT INFORMATION: GOD TAKES THE INITIATIVE TO REVEAL HIMSELF

The culture we grow up in forms our minds and the way we perceive reality. We come to believe that 'the way we do things in our culture' is the way things ought to be done when they're done right. We tend not to see any reason to evaluate our own culture critically unless a compelling alternative is presented. I've met people who have grown up for example in Sweden, China, Iran and the United States who firmly believe that those from other countries/cultures are less developed or less 'cultural' than they are. It would seem that it is only as we encounter other cultures than our own for an extended period of time that people are able to appraise their own culture from a new perspective.

Similarly, in order for anyone to be able to look beyond sin and rebellion against God in their own culture and personal life God needs to break in and challenge their understanding of reality. That is what He did to Abraham and that is what He does through the preaching of the Gospel to all nations today.

Abraham did not receive a theological treatise about God; instead he received a personal call through an unusual revelation of God, a theophany, and he was called to act in faith on the word of God: "Now the LORD said to Abram, 'Go from your country and your kindred and your father's house to the land that I will show you'" (Genesis 12:1). Even though this was a clear and objective revelation, it would take radical faith to obey it. Abraham needed to take action in a way that would startle all of his friends and relatives, except those who decided to come along. But it was a necessary action, because God was about to start something totally new through Abraham—He was going to change the direction of history for all eternity.

This is real prophecy and later in this chapter we will see that the prophesies were not a construction after the events had happened.

GOD'S PURPOSE IS TO BLESS

When God calls on people to believe in Him and to change the direction of their lives, it is in order to bless them and for them to become a blessing to others. That can only be done as they desire to live in fellowship with Him, to listen to His guidance and be led and empowered by His Spirit. There are two things that stand out in this context.

First, it is clear that God did not call Abraham because He needed His help to accomplish His purposes. God, as He reveals Himself in Biblical history, is free to do whatever pleases Him, and He always does that in ways that are in harmony with His holy character. We might never know why He chose Abraham and not somebody else, but as the story continues it is obvious that it is God who makes Abraham great. Through that, Abraham and his descendants discover God's greatness, faithfulness and love for those who want to live in harmony with the way He created the world.

Second, when God called Abraham in order to bless him, He had as His ultimate purpose to bless all nations on the earth. God's blessings for believers are never an end in themselves. Abraham and others who followed do, of course, experience the blessing and moments of glory, but this is often the result of how they related to the hardship and serious challenges the journey involved, and the rewards were not for them only. Like some military victories won by a few, these victories blessed people far and wide. In the same way as God does not act selfishly (what could He gain from tiny humans living on a miniature planet in the vast cosmos anyway?) so His people are called to look beyond themselves and their time to consider others around them as well as future generations.

IT TAKES DARING FAITH

Abraham had to take a radical step of faith. This step came from a clear and objective revelation by God, a theophany. God reveals Himself to us in many ways but a theophany is a rare revelation in critical situations, when God appears in human form. There are only a few instances of it recorded in the Bible.

Abraham would have to trust God for every step of the fulfillment of these long-term promises for the future.

Abraham's radical step of faith to believe was not a leap of faith in the dark, and cannot and should not be followed literally by anyone else because a theophany is meant for a specific individual in a specific situation. For others reading or hearing about it, only time will tell whether it was a real theophany or a delusion. But we know the end of the story for Abraham and can see it was an opportunity for Abraham to discover the character and power of God.

Revelation of God is always tied to a fulfillment in historical reality. It is not just abstract, esoteric information, but is a part of the way God actualizes history in general, and salvation history in particular. Prophetic revelation from God, as it is presented in the Bible, is falsifiable. That has two implications: a prophet in Old Testament-times who spoke in the name of God without the promise coming true was a false prophet who should be executed. That would also be true of a prophet who preached, or spoke things that were in clear contradiction to the verified prophets like Abraham and Moses. As the totality of the Biblical message is meant to be falsifiable, it also means that people hearing and reading it can be held responsible for accepting or rejecting the message.

The flip-side of this means that Biblical revelation is open to scrutiny. It is not a sin to ask questions about revelation, like is sometimes done in some other religious contexts. The sin, and it is a very serious one, is to reject that clear and objective truth presented in the Bible. It is the same level of sin as rejecting the revelation of God in nature, as described in Romans 1.

THE PROMISE TO ABRAHAM

When God called Abraham through a clear and objective theophany, He promised him four things as a reward (that is the word that God actually uses) for his faith.

THE PROMISE OF A SON (GENESIS 12:1; 15:3)

The first promise is that Abraham would have a son. Abraham was 75 years old at the time of the promise and he would have to wait another 25 years before Isaac, the promised son, would be born. God's blessing is more often than not experienced on a long-term basis, which is one of the reasons why we often struggle to believe that His promises actually do come true. Abraham himself was rather confused and asked God if He actually meant what He had said; he even attempted to help God fulfill the promise.

Faith does not seem to imply that Abraham, or we ourselves, won't ever feel forgotten or that we won't misunderstand and make wrong choices. That is a part of the reality of living in a fallen world. God often works under the surface of what the culture of the time is aware of. It was this way in the case of Abraham. Most people who did not have access to the reality of God's revelation to Abraham probably thought he was mistaken, as did Sarah, his wife. There is no hint, however, of a rebuke from God or embarrassment for Abraham. The promise was from God and God took full responsibility to make it come true. We must not forget then, when we think of God's promises to us, that there was a 25-year wait for Abraham until the son was born.

THE PROMISE OF A NATION (GENESIS 12:1)

The second promise was that Abraham would be the father of a nation. If the first promise took time to be fulfilled and was a real faith-challenge, then imagine the faith needed for the second promise. If we had lived at the time of Abraham, Isaac and Jacob we would have probably thought that the second step would never happen, considering the irrational choices of the little embryonic family that was around at the time. Isaac and his wife Rebecca were not able to have children until Isaac prayed to God for help, echoing the story of Abraham and Sarah. God answered Isaac's prayer and they had twins, Jacob and Esau. But the two brothers did not get along, the younger cheating their father for the right to be counted as the firstborn, fleeing the wrath of his twin, and was then in turn cheated by his future father-in-law, marrying two women and also having children with two servant girls. One of his sons slept with one of his father's servant girls, a number of the brothers murdered all the men in a neighboring village, and most of them hated their little brother Joseph so much that they wanted to murder him too, but sold him instead as a slave to Egypt. That is what we today would call a dysfunctional family.

To make matters worse from Jacob's perspective, there came a severe drought and famine to the area where they lived, so severe that they had to buy food from Egypt. It is at this lowest-of-low points that Jacob discovers that Joseph, whom he thought was dead for many years, was not only alive, but had become a high official in Egypt and was now inviting Jacob and his whole family to come to Egypt to live under his protection. God loves mind-blowing story-lines.

There is a meta-story built into the text, which becomes clearer as we discover how the God of Abraham blessed Joseph through all the grim and challenging years after his brothers sold him, how God protected him and orchestrated circumstances around him so that he was not only promoted to be an assistant to the Egyptian Pharaoh, but also became the person through whom the descendants of Abraham survived and became the great nation that God had promised. There are at least two levels of activity in the text. One is about human failure and incapacity to make God's promises come through. The other story is about how God leads and sees to it that His covenants are fulfilled. Only if we know the beginning of the story, going back a few generations, are we able to stand back and recognize these two parallel realities.

THE PROMISE OF A LAND (GENESIS 15)

There was a long time in Abraham's life when fulfillment of the next promise looked very unrealistic. But one day God spoke again to Abraham and not only promised him a son and a nation, but also a geographically delineated area. It would also take a defined period of time before it was going to happen, such a long time that Abraham would have no chance of influencing the way it would happen. It is an understatement to say that the promise was very specific. Take a look at this:

God spoke to Abraham in a revelation that symbolized a solemn covenant ceremony, but on this occasion only one party was making the covenant: God. Walking between pieces of a slaughtered animal communicated that "may what happened to this animal, happen to me if I break this covenant." The flaming fire, that expressed the presence of God, did just that!

God told Abraham that his descendants would live under harsh conditions for four hundred years before the land would be theirs. One day the hard days would come to an end, and the land promised to them would be released to them. Genesis 15 tells this: "On that day the LORD made a covenant with Abram, saying, 'To your offspring I give this land, from the river of Egypt to the great river, the river Euphrates, the land of the Kenites, the Kenizzites, the Kadmonites, the Hittites, the Perizzites, the Rephaim, the Amorites, the Canaanites, the Girgashites and the Jebusites'" (Genesis 15:18–21).

The promise is more than a simple promise. It introduces a number of factors involved: one is that the promise is not conditional on Abraham's efforts, but only on his faith. God tells Abraham that he would die in old age, and his descendants would be granted the land long after that.

The delay was clearly defined to four hundred years, which is the time from when the promise was given to the time when the people of Israel began to enter the Promised Land.

Abraham's family would be afflicted for those four hundred years. From the context we understand that the affliction, in this case, was not something that God necessarily sent over them, but probably a consequence of living with a Divine purpose and favor in a fallen, dysfunctional world.

One more layer of information is that the land would be taken from the nations that lived there and given to Israel because of the iniquity of the nations. The promise presupposes that the sins of those nations would reach satiated levels and that they thereby would forfeit their right to inhabit it. A sobering thought as we see this would be applied later to Israel as well. Hearing this promise from God's timeless perspective, Abraham understood that the two, seemingly disparate historic events (the 400-year wait and the nations that would be displaced because of their sin), were synchronized. But it would happen in a way that could only be perceived if one had prophetic information from God.

The period of affliction would last four hundred years. The Israelites were eventually enslaved by the Egyptians, due in part to the evil in the world in general and in particular because of racism in Egypt at the time. This would end in severe punishment of the oppressors and significant wealth for Israel. We even see how the evil and ungodly acts of racism, idolatry and oppression in Egypt actually mobilized the Israeli national identity. Genesis does in no way suggest that the evil of Egypt or the nations in the promised land was God's will, but it does without any doubt show us how God has full control of history on all levels, and overrules any human attempt to thwart His purposes. He even turns the attacks from unbelievers into blessings.

THE PROMISE THAT ABRAHAM WOULD BE A GLOBAL BLESSING (GENESIS 12:3)

The Fourth Promise

God called Abraham to follow Him in order to bless him with concrete things that would be his in the future: a son, a nation and a land. But there was one more aspect, and that was to make Abraham himself a blessing to all nations. After the fall of Adam humanity decided to try to run their lives on their own, as gods. They acted no more as the representatives and servants of the Lord God Almighty, but drifted into violence, wickedness and idolatry. The same thing happened after the cataclysmic judgment of the flood. An early illustration of this rebellion was the building of the tower of Babel, which most likely was a ziggurat, a temple-tower where the top part was dedicated to an idol. Abraham's own family were idol worshippers, so when God calls on Abraham to leave his land and clan it was to begin something new, great and history changing.

In living by faith Abraham was going to be a catalyst for world change. The strategy for accomplishing this was to continue to live by faith in God and in obedience to Him. God would be in charge of how it would happen and Abraham would trust. Although Abraham couldn't foresee all that would happen he did understand that it was a blessing that would be far greater than anything he could ever grasp at the time.

Since that is the backstory of God's call and blessing, it makes sense that anyone who blessed Abraham would also be blessed, because that person or that nation would be joining in on God's purpose to bless the nations. On the other hand, those who would try to put obstacles in the way or even curse or dishonor Abraham would be fighting against God's intention to bless all nations, and would therefore be cursed and/or dishonored by God.

God created the people of Israel to be a witness to the person and purposes of God, to be a light to the nations by trusting Him and living under His provision. In this day, we can now see that the main purpose of the Law of the Old Testament was also to prepare that nation for the coming of the Messiah/Christ. Throughout the Bible this is understood as a necessary stage towards the ultimate fulfillment of Abraham's promise. Although everything did not happen in an exemplary way, the Old Testament is one great call to Israel to live the way God called them to live and to be a light to the nations.

Even though the Israelites often were more influenced by the nations they were called to influence than the other way around, God did not rescind on His promise. In spite of Israel's unbelief, God continued to work. Those Israelites who did not believe and follow God did not experience the personal benefits of the promise, but were more like mail deliverers who themselves do not know the content of what they deliver. Those who did believe continued to live under the same blessing that was given to Abraham, and a considerable group was ready to see and welcome what God was doing at the arrival of Jesus Christ.

The early church understood that the blessing promised to Abraham was available to anyone from any nation who believed and accepted what God had promised. When the apostles taught this, they did not invent something new, but just brought to light what God time and time again had promised through the Old Testament prophets. The promise of a nation was of course fulfilled as the nation of Israel was born and liberated from Egyptian slavery. But that was only the beginning. God had a great future for the nation of Israel: that all nations would come to faith in God and that God's glory would be manifest throughout the earth, as was His original intention in Eden. This is being fulfilled today and the rate of growth of those who thank God for Abraham's faith increases dramatically year by year. More on this in the next chapter.

WHAT ABOUT TODAY?

The fulfillment of God's promise to Abraham is still happening today, right before our eyes. It might be politically incorrect to claim this, but it is nonetheless true. The nation of Israel today is a clear and dramatic reminder that the God of Abraham, Isaac and Jacob works to fulfill His purposes through all generations.

The promise to Abraham about a people, nation and being a blessing, was given about four thousand years ago. The oldest complete Genesis manuscript is found in Codex Alexandrinus from the 5th Century AD. There are fragments of Genesis found in the Dead Sea Scrolls (1QGen) from at least 100 BC that tell us that the later manuscripts represent the original content faithfully.

We are the first generation in almost 2000 years that can watch God fulfilling His promise to Abraham. Christians who have understood the Bible in a Historical-Grammatical way (that means that they try to understand the Bible through a normal, non-speculative reading) have always expected the return of the nation of Israel from the diaspora, but most of them never lived to see it happen. That changed in 1948. The land was promised by God Himself to Abraham and it would take some ingenious thought processes to explain that promise away.

The return of the nation of Israel does not mean that God approves of everything the government of the state of Israel does. That has never been the case and there have in fact been long periods when the prophets have had to rebuke the people and call them to repent and turn to God in faith and obedience. The same is true today, and it should not at all surprise us. What should surprise is that so many Jews and Christians talk as though Israel is by default exempt from acting justly. Anyone who has read the Bible knows that it is most certainly not the case.

The point of the argument is that God has worked in a way that is hidden from the wisdom of this world in order to fulfill His promise to Abraham. It is not because one nation is more noble than others. It is because God decided to use the nation of Israel as an agent of salvation to the world, like He did at the coming of Christ and the birth of the Church.

This reality is a big challenge to all of us who were brought up to think with a Western mindset. It just does not seem to make sense, and it messes up how we think about the political situation in the Middle East. There is no way today we can cleverly negotiate peace in the international conflict in the Middle East, and yet many Christians and most secular persons prefer to ignore what God has said will happen and what He will do in this area. As will be shown later in the book, God's promises are much more exciting and transforming than choosing sides in the conflict.

To anyone who is interested in the reality of what the promises say and who is open to the fact that God works in a far more intricate way than we could ever possibly understand, the metastory is obvious: God is there, He makes promises to people who want to live under His blessing and we can be sure that He brings about what He promised. The evidence is overwhelming. The invitation to live under God's blessing did not end with the rebellion and fall of the first humans. God Himself did not change when they fell. He still intends to lead history forward to fulfill His purposes and He is doing that in and through people who are willing to have faith in Him, like Abraham.

But there are more arguments to ponder—ones we've habituated to such an extent that we no longer perceive the obvious. The arguments have to do with the growth of Biblically based Christian churches and the persecution of the Church.

Chapter 4

Follow the Signs—The Church

In this chapter I aim to show that:

1. God promised Abraham that he would be a blessing to all nations. That was 4000 years ago
2. Jesus, the descendant of Abraham, told His disciples that all nations would be impacted by the preaching of the Gospel. That was 2000 years ago
3. It took 1900 years for the Church to encompass 10 percent of the Global population
4. Since then, the growth of the confessing Church is so strong that it is a powerful reminder of the reliability of the Bible

THE GREAT SURPRISE

When I had just decided to go into ministry, years ago, a concerned friend asked me to reconsider, because he could not see any career opportunities in a dying church. Growing up in rural northern Sweden, I was unfamiliar with the idea of 'career opportunities', and I must admit, it didn't concern me much. I just wanted to do what I thought was right at the time and I had absolutely no idea of what was happening globally. I was interested but ignorant about what God was doing in the world. Since then I have discovered that the Church is now growing faster than during any other era in history.

The beginning of the Church that Jesus foretold came at a time and in a manner that God was fully in charge of in His sovereign way. The timing of this came as a surprise to most of His contemporaries who had no way of understanding the significance of what had happened to the Jesus they had recently seen crucified. The manner in which the Church began came as a surprise to everybody, including the first disciples. All they knew was that what happened on the day of Pentecost was so clearly a direct work of God that Peter and the other disciples immediately interpreted what happened in a Biblical context. Since that time, the Church has grown and spread throughout the world, but, astonishingly, the most intense growth to date began in the early 1900s. The growth in the last 100 years is not a fluke of history. In fact, before His crucifixion Jesus predicted that this exact thing would happen. The principle of Biblical prophecy is that the word should be followed with a historical fact. In this case, the words of Jesus are fulfilled right before our eyes. This confirmation should challenge us to believe the rest of what He said about the future.

I have been in ministry for a long time as an educator and pastor, and I'm fairly certain that when it comes to the church I have seen it all—the good, the bad and the ugly—believe me. On the positive end, my wife and I have had the privilege of knowing many Christians who are true saints. Some of them were not very religious types, but they loved God and were committed followers of Jesus. One of these was my predecessor when I pastored a small church in the town where our two daughters grew up and where I believe we experienced true community. In our little church there were theologians, carpenters, shop-keepers, nurses, students, factory workers and business executives who came together to worship God, serve each other and the community. Our daughters came to regard many of them as heroes who had earned the right to be emulated.

God and the Spiritual Tsunami

I will never forget a theological conversation I had with that predecessor. He was an eighty year-old man who exuded kindness and humor, while commanding the respect of someone who might have been taught by the apostles themselves. We discussed one aspect of baptism and we had a friendly, minor disagreement. A couple of days later we met again and, to my great surprise, he told me that he had read up on the subject and had come to the conclusion that I was right. It honestly did not matter to me who was right but I remember how humbled I felt when this old man was willing to concede. The impact was that I promised myself to try to be like that towards those younger than myself as I grew older.

I have also seen the other side, when leaders have cheated, lied, sinned and played power games. One of my very first memories from an early church experience was two grown church men getting into a fist fight over a minor budget issue. It is only by God's grace that I still am a believer. I love the Church more than ever, but it is not because of the witness of the Church that I believe. I belong to the Church because I believe in Jesus, and I am just one of the many Church members in need of continued grace and protection from Jesus—the One who builds His Church.

A GLOBAL GOD-MOVEMENT

It might well surprise many to learn that we live in the most expansive era of the Church in history. It is a time that can only be compared to the first generation of Christians. Here, I need to add the caveat that I define "the Church" as I believe the New Testament does: those fellowships of believers—regardless of denominational affiliation—who believe the historic Christian message. The message is that Jesus is the Son of God, that he performed the miracles that the Bible ascribes to Him, that He died and bodily rose from the dead on the third day, that the Holy Spirit works in the world today to fill and empower followers of Jesus to serve Him. According to past and current research, the Church based on this message grows fast and convincingly. The Church, of course, includes all who believe the historic message and who belong to the traditional denominations, but it is not confined to those, or any one group.

Sadly, in Europe and the USA, the Church does not look all that impressive. Here Church growth is the slowest. But do not let that fool you. The Church grows exponentially in some of the most hostile environments in the world. In China, for instance, it has been growing so rapidly that the Communist government does all it can to hinder it, without success.

When the Communist Party took power in China the Church had half a million members, and they were treated with suspicion and persecution. During the so-called Cultural Revolution persecution increased aggressively and to some it looked like the Church in China was being wiped out. But that was not going to be the case. If the present rate of growth continues, there might well be around 250 million Christians in China by the year 2030. Astonishingly, that would make China the country with the largest Christian community in the world.

I will never forget a teaching-weekend for local church leaders in China. I travelled together with a friend who had visited these places earlier. The week-end was attended by one hundred full-time pastors and evangelists from a church that did not 'exist'. Those leaders represented a total of ten thousand members. During that weekend we were visited by three leaders from another province and I noticed that one of them had his baseball cap on all the time. When we met more privately he took off his cap and showed us his prisoner's hair-cut. He had been released from prison just a few days earlier. I asked him how many members there were in his province that related to his particular denomination. He avoided answering my question and I could not understand why, until I realized that he did not want to seem boastful. After some more, probably very rude, Western probing, he finally answered: "About eleven million."

The growth of the church in China is not just a rumor. It is happening. It scares the wits out of the Communist, atheist government. Above all it is a reminder of how God is fulfilling His promise to Abraham and how Jesus is doing exactly what He said

He would do—build His Church among all nations. "I will build my church, and the gates of Hell will not overcome it" (Matthew 16:18).

The Church in Africa has grown more than 50 percent over the last fifteen years, and more than 30 000 become Christians each day, in Africa alone. Indonesia, the largest Muslim nation in the world, might be a major Christian country within a couple of decades. These are just a few examples. Something extraordinary is happening on planet earth, and the most significant increase began to happen in the beginning of the last century and continues on today.

If you lived in the eighteen hundreds when reductionistic theology (a theology which basically denies miracles) began to be popular, it would have been easy to lose hope. It looked like the church was becoming domesticated and no longer was that great challenge to the unbelieving society. But if you had held on to the credibility of the Bible through this era you would still have had reason to both expect the reappearance of the nation of Israel and the rapid expansion of the Church, because of the simple fact that Jesus said it would happen. Look at the two examples that are found in Matthew and Luke and then make up your own mind.

THE GOSPEL OF MATTHEW

The growth of the Church was foretold by Jesus in Matthew 28. It was after His crucifixion, when it looked like there was no future for the Church He earlier had claimed He would build. He had said (Matt 16:18) ". . .I will build my church. . ." and indicated that He would use Peter to do that. Then came what looked like the disaster of His death. The Christians were soon to discover something that Jesus had told them on numerous occasions: the death of Jesus had been in the plan long before the creation of the universe and it was the only possible way to save mankind from its self-imposed destruction.

After the resurrection, Jesus makes an astounding declaration:

Follow the Signs—The Church

And Jesus came and said to them, "All authority in heaven and on earth has been given to me. Go therefore and make disciples of all nations, baptizing them in the name of the Father and of the Son and of the Holy Spirit, teaching them to observe all that I have commanded you. And behold, I am with you always, to the end of the age" (Matthew 28:18-20).

Let's look at the text step by step.

If it is true that Jesus has "all authority everywhere," it means that He can do whatever He wants, wherever and whenever He wants to do it. It is an absolute, unlimited authority. He does not need anybody's help to do what He wants, but He might invite us to participate in what He plans to do. That is very like Him—it was the way God did it in the beginning of mankind's history. He did not need humans to create the Earth, but He called on them to be His vice-regents.

So, the "therefore" in the text must be read in the context of Jesus having the unlimited ability to do what He wants. We naturally read the next word, "Go" as an imperative or order, and it can easily be taken that way. The original text however is more subtle than that. "Go" is written as a present participle, "Going, therefore" or "as you therefore go. . ." In its immediate context, it probably means that since Jesus has the ultimate authority in the world, anything He says will be done. It also means that the disciples are told to go and do what they are told to, but it includes the thought that they will be led by Jesus to do what they are told to do. It will surely happen! Nothing in the Bible should be understood in a Western, mechanical way. Taken in its context, it means at least two things simultaneously: firstly, God's purposes will be fulfilled, and, secondly, humans have a responsibility to obey and act in faith/obedience.

The disciples task was/is to make disciples of all nations. That is a tall order because Jesus is not telling them to make some disciples from every nation. No, they are to make disciples of all nations. In other words, to disciple all nations. That is a huge difference and impossible to accomplish for anyone, let alone these amateurish fellows who probably hadn't even visited another country before. The enormity of the task looks ludicrous, unless something unforeseen was about to happen.

When he tells them to make disciples of all nations few would believe that he meant one hundred percent of humanity will become disciples. Other parables He told would contradict such a notion. But if He doesn't mean 100%, does He mean 90, or 50 or 20 percent? He does seem to mean that so many from any given nation will become disciples of Christ that it would be fair to say that from now on a particular nation would be considered discipled.

The book of Acts gives us a good indication of what Jesus means. On the day of Pentecost an astounding 3000 were baptized and a short time later there were already 5000 believers in the Jerusalem area. Soon there were so many that the opposition changed from occasional persecution of leaders to a general persecution of Christ-followers. Later, we read that whole cities were in uproar as the Apostles preached. The message of Jesus as Lord became a felt threat by the political and religious leaders. When we read how Jesus tells the twelve to make disciples of all nations, we must understand that in view of all his teaching. He foretold that they would be persecuted because of their faith in Him, and that the persecution will go on until His return.

The picture we get of 'go make disciples of all nations' is therefore one of great impact, that more than just a few were impacted and that the growth was viciously opposed.

The 'method' for the first Christians, and for any of their future followers, to accomplish Jesus' plan was to baptize them in the name of the Triune God; that does of course imply that the converts had first heard the proclaimed message. The picture we get from the Gospels is that Jesus and His disciples proclaimed the message to unbelievers. This word "proclaimed" is incredibly important. The word is used in Matthew and Mark's gospel and means speaking with an authority that brings about the message. Luke's gospel uses the word "evangelize," which was understood very differently from how that word is used today, because it was used in exactly the same way as Matthew and Mark used the word "proclaim": it has a bold, confident and reality-transforming implication. If that fills you with fear and dread, join the club; but it is a word worth wrestling and persevering with. Most of all, remember that its reality can only be realized in our lives (as triumphantly as it should) as we live it out with God's presence and God's help, the One who never leaves us nor forsakes us.

Once people had heard the message, believed and been baptized, they were to be taught everything that Jesus had commanded, and that meant not only truths about God and how to live morally as a believer, but it must have meant that new disciples were to proclaim the Gospel of the Kingdom in a similar way to how Jesus and His first disciples did this.

THE GOSPEL OF LUKE

Luke describes what Jesus said on another occasion after His resurrection in a situation where His disciples had not expected Him to appear, so Luke emphasizes that they were surprised and doubting. Jesus then used the situation to give them a quick overview of what the whole Old Testament is about to show them what was about to happen next. This is what He told them:

As they were talking about these things, Jesus himself stood among them, and said to them, "Peace to you!" But they were startled and frightened and thought they saw a spirit. And he said to them, "Why are you troubled, and why do doubts arise in your hearts? See my hands and my feet, that it is I myself. Touch me, and see. For a spirit does not have flesh and bones as you see that I have." And when he had said this, he showed them his hands and his feet. And while they still disbelieved for joy and were marveling, he said to them, "Have you anything here to eat?" They gave him a piece of broiled fish, and he took it and ate before them. Then he said to them, "These are my words that I spoke to you while I was still with you, that everything written about me in the Law of Moses and the Prophets and the Psalms must be fulfilled." Then he opened their minds to understand the Scriptures, and said to them, "Thus it is written, that the Christ should suffer and on the third day rise from the dead, and that repentance and forgiveness of sins should be proclaimed in his name to all nations, beginning from Jerusalem. You are witnesses of these things. And behold, I am sending the promise of my Father upon you. But stay in the city until you are clothed with power from on high." (Luke 24:36–49)

Jesus first showed the disciples what the resurrection actually meant. They seemed to be ready to believe that He came as some kind of spiritual apparition, but He quickly showed them that He had risen bodily from the dead, exactly as He had told them He would. They could touch Him, and He ate broiled fish right before their eyes.

He then told them something that was new to them and often hard for 21st Century persons to take to heart as well. His resurrection was not something that should have surprised them, because the resurrection was foretold by the Old Testament prophets, and it is a part of a larger Divine plan, which is to offer salvation to all nations. This is how the Jesus argument goes:

First, they needed to remember that Jesus had told them on numerous occasions that He was going to be killed, but that He would be resurrected. It was absolutely necessary for that to happen, because God had foretold it in the Old Testament, and anything that God had foretold would without a doubt happen. God's word is His declaration of what will happen. One cannot separate God's word from historical reality, because that would produce an empty religion. Jesus staked His whole future on God's promise that He would have to die on a cross but that He would be resurrected on the third day, and His disciples needed to have that same trust in God and His word. The total truth of God's word was not just meant to give believers something to discuss in their spare time, but was to be the guiding revelation for all their important decisions.

So, the Scriptures said that Christ would suffer and be raised again on the third day. Then he continues to remind them that the same Scriptures also said that "repentance and forgiveness of sins should be proclaimed in His name to all nations, beginning from Jerusalem." That promise (as is true of every one of God's promises) is of the same category as the death and resurrection of

Jesus. In other words, the death and resurrection of Jesus shows us the power behind God's promises: ". . .so is my word that goes out from my mouth: It will not return to me empty, but will accomplish what I desire and achieve the purpose for which I sent it" (Isaiah 55:11).

The apostles were witnesses of this. They had seen the first part of God's meta-plan happen, and they were now going to witness how He would begin to implement the second part of it.

Then Jesus gave them a surprising command: He basically told them not to do anything right away. They were instead told to go to Jerusalem, and wait for the next great thing that would happen: they were going to be clothed with power from heaven. God's plan was not to ask unprepared rookies to take on the world on their own. They would soon get the power they needed, but before this they should not try to build the Church on their own.

The way that the world would encounter the Gospel was to meet men and women who lived their lives the same way Jesus did. They were to trust in God's will and power to lead them, to give them the power and the resources they needed and to be willing to do whatever they were told by God to do.

So, Jesus told His disciples that God was about to send the message of "repentance and forgiveness of sins" to be proclaimed in the name of Jesus Christ to all nations. He is talking about nations, not some local phenomenon. His plan is all encompassing.

WHAT IS YOUR VERDICT?

This chapter aims to show how the prophetic character of the Biblical prophecies compels us to look at Jesus Christ.

Four thousand years ago, God promised Abraham that he would have a son and become a people and a nation. He soon had his son but it would take more than four hundred years before all these promises would be fulfilled. However, the promise was given and even a date set. In addition, Abraham would be a blessing to all nations; alternatively it could be read as "all nations would bless themselves" because they had learned about Abraham's blessing.

God and the Spiritual Tsunami

Two thousand years ago, Jesus said that God was going to bring the nations to repentance and faith. Like in the case of Abraham it started small, as with the mustard seed illustration that He Himself told. But it began to grow, starting from Jerusalem, spreading to Judea and Samaria, and then to all the non-Jewish nations. By the year 300 AD it had grown so much that the Roman Empire basically gave in to the Church and step by step incorporated the church to its system. It was probably not a good thing for the church and we must remember that it was not the whole church that succumbed to that incorporation—it led to constant needs for reform and revival. But there was definitely significant dynamic growth during the first centuries.

The church (by that I mean all denominations) had, by the year 1900 AD, roughly grown to include about 10% of the global population. By then a foundation had been laid by the Moravian, Methodist and Reformed revivals that provided a fresh vision for the Church. Then, in the beginning of the 1900s something happened. Larger numbers of Christians than before began to experience the dynamic realities of the Christian faith. The presence of the Holy Spirit was not something totally new. Similar things had happened before. But now it spread faster and was not to be contained in any one denominational structure. A global revival started and the growth of the Church has exploded and continues on today. Hundreds of new churches are planted every day, and new converts are counted in the thousands. Cultures and nations are being changed. We live in the most dynamic era of the Church since the time of the Apostles. No group has control over the growth. It goes beyond denominational boundaries. It bypasses some of the older Western denominations that once looked upon themselves as the guarantors of the faith but have succumbed to a reductionistic theology that the first generation of Christians would not recognize. The Church is by no means dying.

All this means that our generation is the first generation that with our own eyes is witnessing how God fulfills His promise to Abraham and how Jesus made it all possible by His death, resurrection and ascension. One has to choose to be stone-blind to miss this.

In Chapter Three we saw how the Bible is shown to be relevant and true because God does what He promised to Israel and always fulfills what He says. In Chapter Four we have seen how this is relevant and true because of the reality of the promised expansion of the church in the world. The next step—and this is somewhat surprising—we will see that Jesus foretold that His followers will be persecuted, but that this persecution is not something to dread because it will provide far more opportunities to be a witness about faith in Jesus Christ.

Chapter 5

Follow the Signs: Turning Persecution to Victory

In this chapter I aim to show that:

1. Jesus prepared His disciples for the coming persecution
2. The early Christians experienced this persecution. It has continued throughout the ages
3. It goes on today and it is the greatest attack on human rights today
4. History indicates that God will honor those who follow Him in persecution and their ministry will bear fruit in a remarkable and surprising way
5. Jesus told His disciples that they would be persecuted. And they were persecuted, from the early days of the Church to today, when it is worse than ever

PERSECUTION IS NOT THE END

If you stand out, there is a good chance that you will meet resistance from those whose status is challenged because of you. Some will even react simply because their status quo is perceived as being threatened. No one should be surprised that persecution of those who think differently is going on all over the world, openly or subtly. Jesus told His disciples that they would be persecuted. And they were, from the early days of the Church to today, when it is worse than ever.

Persecution is not the end, though. God, who has not promised to protect us from persecution, has emphatically promised to be with us in persecution. The growth of the Church and its persecution is a powerful sign of the credibility of the Scriptures. Ultimately this will reveal the power of God to keep His promises to believers. With time it will also reveal, mercilessly, the folly of the persecutors.

PERSECUTION FORETOLD

My friend and I met with a Chinese pastor who had not been able to go home for more than two years, because the police were watching his house to arrest him. He was not a criminal, just a Christian pastor who would rather die than compromise his faith. The little church he started had grown to become a house church movement of more than one million members. That is one of the 'smaller' movements by Chinese standards. We met somewhere in the countryside. We were just taken there, and we asked no questions about our destination. Leaders from all over the enormous country had gathered. Some had traveled by train more than three days. The atmosphere was full of faith. No hard words against the police or the government were said, but the kindness was entwined with an absolute commitment to be Christ-followers, regardless of the cost. It seemed as though persecution fosters leaders who can love their enemies, and not be afraid of them in the least. One national leader told us: "They have arrested and imprisoned me, beaten me, taken my money, cameras and laptops so many times now, so I don't even know what it means to be afraid anymore."

He and a minister from Europe were once arrested and interrogated. Because of some mysterious intervention from someone higher up in the Chinese bureaucracy they were let out of the arrest after a day, with strict orders not to preach again. As soon as they were out on the street the national leader told my friends: "I want you to meet the church in such-and-such a city." They went there, ministered, encouraged the believers, and my friend discovered that there was a large number of churches in that city too. Instead of persecution stopping the growth of the church it seems to be like gasoline thrown on fire. These Christians know that most of the time persecution comes as a side-effect of powerful and effective ministry that by its very essence threatens the status quo in society, and they are more than willing to pay the price for the world to encounter the reality of Jesus Christ.

JESUS WAS THE FIRST MARTYR IN THE NEW TESTAMENT

Jesus did not only promise that His church would be spread throughout the earth, but also that it would be persecuted in the harshest possible way. How is this as an assurance for the fledgling disciples?

> 12 . . . they will lay their hands on you and persecute you, delivering you up to the synagogues and prisons, and you will be brought before kings and governors for my name's sake.
>
> 13 This will be your opportunity to bear witness.
>
> . . .16 You will be delivered up even by parents and brothers and relatives and friends, and some of you they will put to death.
>
> 17 You will be hated by all for my name's sake.
>
> 18 But not a hair of your head will perish. Luke 21:12–18

This is exactly what happened. It all began with Jesus Himself who, time and time again, told His followers that He would be arrested, killed and after that, resurrected on the third day. It did not make sense to the disciples, and they needed to see that whole scenario disclosed before they partly got it. In the same way, persecution of the followers of Jesus still does not make sense to the

Western mind. It is not until we begin to accept the fact that we live in a fallen, dysfunctional world that we see that Jesus' teaching makes sense. Persecution seems to be a necessary part of the life of the global Church.

The reason Jesus was crucified was that He did the will of God the Father in full obedience and in a perfect way. The rebellion against God is so deep-rooted that the person who consistently lives in a different way will stir up frustration and anger to such a degree that it will lead to persecution. The lifestyle of a God follower will be felt as a serious threat to the system of the world. Once again: it might sound counter-intuitive, but this is still the case. Jesus was the first one to experience it. Then came Stephen, James, eleven of the twelve Apostles, Polycarp, Jan Hus, John Wycliffe, Thomas Cramner, William Tyndall together with tens of thousands of others in different parts of the world. It still goes on.

Jesus became a challenge to the religious leaders in Jerusalem because they saw Him as a threat to their own position of power. They feared that so many would accept Jesus' claims that they themselves would lose influence. They also saw Jesus as a heretic who did not accept the traditional understanding of the Old Testament. Thirdly, they were afraid that the Romans would react to any large disturbance that Jesus' followers could create and that the Romans would outlaw worship at the Temple, or worse, just tear it down. These aspects created a situation that they felt was out of their control.

The Romans, on their part, had at most a vague understanding of who Jesus was. But they believed that Jesus's claim of being the King of God's new Kingdom might be seen as rebellion against the Emperor in Rome. That was reason enough for them to sentence Him to crucifixion, a Roman method of execution.

The absolute claims of Jesus put the proponents of the existing order in a difficult, if not impossible, situation. Their choice seemed to be either to accept the claims of Jesus or to use brute force to stop Him. The use of arguments would not be effective. How can mere arguments prevail over someone who raises the dead? Jesus understood this from the beginning. He saw the world through the eyes of Old Testament teaching and prepared His followers for what was bound to happen.

STEPHEN THE MARTYR WAS NEXT . . .

The first martyrs were killed in Jerusalem. The first one was named Stephen, one of the early leaders and administrators of the Church. Not only was he an able administrator, he could also proclaim the message, and he did that accompanied by powerful signs and wonders.

The Christian faith is not a status quo alternative. Truth can never be expected to preserve the status quo, unless we live in a perfectly good and fully enlightened world. The message of Jesus claims to be true, but Jesus' example prohibits his followers from forcing these convictions on others. He was willing to die for the truth, but not use force to defend Himself or His teaching. Still the claim of historic Christianity is that it tells the truth and nothing but the truth, and it is God's truth. That is in itself too much to stomach for a lot of people.

THE SOCIAL ORDER REPS, THE TROUBLE MAKERS AND THE RELIGIOUS EXTREMISTS

The representatives of the existing order in society tried to reason and argue with Stephen. We may think it should be possible to reason about faith and religion, but that presupposes that society is committed to free discussion and free will and that any group is willing to lose influence when people move their allegiance to another group. This is seldom the case.

Not only was it impossible to negotiate with Stephen who told the truth and was filled with wisdom and power from the Holy Spirit—an uneven level of debate in itself. He also performed "great wonders and signs." It does seem reasonable to expect a person who claims to have the truth to have something to show for it, and Stephen certainly had that. From the context in the book of

Follow the Signs: Turning Persecution to Victory

Acts we understand that "great wonders and signs" meant that sick people were healed and demon oppressed or possessed persons were freed.

The logic at the time was that the only way to stop the message was to use force. Most of the Apostles were arrested and later executed, and Stephen paid for his claim of speaking the truth by being stoned to death. Arguments did not work on him so they had to kill him, if they were to protect the old order that was in rebellion to God (which they would have refused to acknowledge, as they would have thought of it as the other way around). They were caught in their own system and convinced themselves that they were doing the right thing.

Jesus understood this clearly and prepared Himself, as well as His disciples, for the persecution that would come. As in the case of Stephen, the representatives of the old system had to kill Jesus. It does not matter if they were Jewish or Roman; they had to yield or act in defense but towards their own moral defeat. Ironically, their lives were never in jeopardy, because Jesus and His disciples were not trying to introduce an alternative political order, and yet the threat was perceived to be so very serious that the defenders of the existing order mobilized. Jesus and the disciples just told the truth, and then history unfolded in the way that God had foretold by the prophets.

There was a second group of persecutors, and these kinds of people are always around: the bullies. They are the people who are threatened by, and therefore hate, anything they're not used to. They are ready to be used by others to lie in court, like some did in the case of Stephen, or to stir up a riot, as some did when Paul preached in Ephesus. Some are just troublemakers, ready to join anything that uses violence against anyone. These people have always been around, and are still around, all over the world.

The persecutors are ready to twist facts, like they did in the case of Stephen. Jesus had said that even if some destroyed the Temple He would raise it up in three days. At His trial some thugs swore that they had heard him say that He Himself would destroy the Temple. With time, that false rumor became the accepted truth in Jerusalem. Then Stephen was accused of being a follower of Jesus. This is what has happened throughout history. Lies were used against the first Christians during the early persecutions, during the Middle Ages when both heretics and evangelicals were persecuted, and it is so to this day. Just listen to some political discourses and media presentations about believing Christians today. Most of those who participate in the genocide against Christians in the Middle East have no idea what Christians believe, but they have heard and bought into distortions.

Then there is a third group of persecutors, the Zealots. The Apostle Paul had been one of them. They are the religious extremists who cannot stand the thought that their personal faith system is being questioned or criticized. They honestly believe that heresy must be rooted out, and if violence is needed, so be it. They are what I call the "well-informed dis-informed." They believe they know much about their own system of thoughts, but are poorly informed about the belief content of those they dislike.

When these three groups collude, we have the necessary conditions in place for the perfect storm of persecution. Anyone not in full agreement will be persecuted by someone. It has always happened, and, sadly, it is the state of the world. It does not help to deny this and behave like the problem is not there.

In regard to the followers of Jesus, they have been duly warned by their Lord that if they take their faith seriously they will be persecuted.

IT CONTINUES . . .

Severe persecution happened in France after the 1789 revolution, in Mexico around the 1900s, in Soviet Russia, China and many other places. It still goes on and is on the increase, especially after the so called Arab Spring.

What we see today is a level of persecution that seems to exceed even the time of Nero. More Christians are killed for their faith today than during any other time in history. The estimate is that between 10,000 to 100,000 Christians were killed over 300 years before 313 AD, Nero and Diocletian being the worst offenders. The religious freedom organization Open Doors estimates that 3000 persons were killed in 2015 alone and the pressure increases.

To many this sounds alarming and scary, while it is seen as something quite normal by other Christians. There was a remarkable interview with Pope Tawadros II, the leader of the Coptic Church, after the beheading of 21 Christians by ISIS; he said: "If there were no martyrs, the right faith could not be delivered to us to the current day and forever. . ." During another interview he said that the church should always be ready to give martyrs to the world. "It makes no difference whether they be Catholics, Orthodox, Copts or Protestants," the Pope continued. "They are Christians! Their blood is one and the same. Their blood confesses Christ."

That is an extraordinary world view, and gives us an insight into the reality of Christians' lives in other parts of the world than our own.

The present martyrs remind us, among other things, that what Jesus told in the Bible, about being persecuted for faith in God, is to be taken seriously. Together with the reality of Israel, the growth of the Church and the present very active persecution, any abstract faith discussions lose their attraction, and we are forced to align our lives with His word or reject it.

> 8 And Stephen, full of grace and power, was doing great wonders and signs among the people.
>
> 9 Then some of those who belonged to the synagogue of the Freedmen (as it was called), and of the Cyrenians, and of the Alexandrians, and of those from Cilicia and Asia, rose up and disputed with Stephen.
>
> 10 But they could not withstand the wisdom and the Spirit with which he was speaking.
>
> 11 Then they secretly instigated men who said, "We have heard him speak blasphemous words against Moses and God."

12 And they stirred up the people and the elders and the scribes, and they came upon him and seized him and brought him before the council,

13 and they set up false witnesses who said, "This man never ceases to speak words against this holy place and the law,

14 for we have heard him say that this Jesus of Nazareth will destroy this place and will change the customs that Moses delivered to us." (Acts 6)

PERSECUTION IS ALWAYS WRONG, BUT GOD WILL TURN THE DEVIL'S WEAPONS AGAINST HIM

Persecution is evil, ineffective and ends up disclosing the stupidity of the perpetrators. The religious leaders who wanted Jesus crucified are shown to be corrupt. Pilate who ordered the crucifixion looks indecisive and cowardly. The group that stoned Stephen was irrational and extremist. And the contemporary persecutors—be they Communists, Middle Eastern terrorists or secular fanatics—alienate most people, and only a few (very disillusioned, psychologically disturbed or extremely naive), would ever want to be associated with them. Not only are these people fighting against God, which is a very unwise idea, but they are unwittingly fighting against their own cause.

When Jesus told his disciples that they would meet persecution he also added some remarkable promises. The first promise was that the persecution would provide them with opportunities to witness to the Gospel (Luke 21:13). In the context it seems to imply that even though persecution is evil in itself, the disciples would be able to look beyond the suffering and deprecation and look for a higher, mature way to respond. They would find themselves talking to people that they would never have had a chance to meet by themselves, and by responding in the way they did, and by just telling the truth, they would serve the higher purpose.

Later, in the same passage (v17–18) Jesus tells them that they will be hated by all for his sake, but after having told them that some of them would even be killed he promised: "... not a hair of your head will perish." That is obviously not a populist way of calling future leaders of the Church, but it did make complete sense to Jesus' disciples. They might get themselves in so much trouble that they would be killed, but God's purpose for their lives would not be thwarted. Everything that God had promised them would happen. They were called to proclaim the faith, they would have to suffer, but the Church would be spread throughout the earth, their lives would matter and they would one day be resurrected with Jesus and be fully vindicated. That is the way they and thousands of martyrs have reasoned. They think: "I might die, but I will not be defeated."

The Apostle Paul expresses this kind of faith in the Epistle to the Philippians, a letter that he wrote while he was in prison. He writes that what has happened to him has led to the advance of the Gospel. The imperial guard had been made aware that Paul was imprisoned because he preached Christ. Furthermore, other leaders who watched Paul being persecuted were emboldened, so they also preached more. Even some of Paul's enemies saw his imprisonment as an opportunity to create a platform for themselves. That was not a very good reason, but Paul says that even if they didn't like him, at least they preached Christ. How can you stop a movement with leaders like this?

One of the early Church leaders, Tertullian, wrote that "the blood of the martyrs is seed of the church." The more you persecute these people, the bolder they become and they will be instrumental in leading even more people to faith in Jesus. In perspective, we see that this was true of the early church.

The persecution of Christians led to more preaching. Nonbelievers watched and were both impressed and convicted by the bold faith of the early Church. There was also a less visible result: even though many became Christians they did not do so because it was a popular movement with shallow promises of an easy life. They joined a despised movement because of inner conviction.

God and the Spiritual Tsunami

That formed a stronger church which was not free from problems, misunderstandings and sometimes questionable theology, but the Christians were in there for the long haul and were willing to follow Jesus in the midst of repression.

A LONG TERM PERSPECTIVE ON PERSECUTION

The Czech Church reformer and martyr Jan (John) Hus is a telling example of how God can turn evil into something good for the world. He was born around 1372 and was burned to death in 1415. He was a priest, philosopher, and, for a time, the rector of the University of Prague. He was influenced by the English reformer John Wycliffe and became one of the early reformers of the Church.

He began to criticize the moral decline of the clergy, including the bishops and even the pope, and his teaching developed into something that has been received both by Protestants and many Orthodox. Well, he was excommunicated, and in spite of assurances of safe conduct to a Church council in Constance, he was arrested and burned at the stake in 1415. At his execution he said: "You might roast this goose (Hus means 'goose') but in one hundred years a swan will sing, and him you will not be able to stop."

Poggius Florentini was a Roman Catholic priest and an observer at Huss' martyrdom. As an eye-witness he wrote about all that happened.

> "In thee, O Lord, I put my trust, bow down thine ear to me." With such Christian prayers, Hus arrived at the stake, looking at it without fear. He climbed upon it, after two assistants of the hangman had torn his clothes from him and had clad him into a shirt drenched with pitch. At that moment, one of the electors, Prince Ludwig of the Palatinate, rode up and pleaded with Hus to recant, so that he might be spared a death in the flames. But Hus replied: "Today you will roast a lean goose, but hundred years from now you will hear a swan sing, whom you

will leave unroasted and no trap or net will catch him for you." Full of pity and filled with much admiration, the Prince turned away[1].

The prophecy was about Martin Luther (whose family emblem was the swan) long before the reformer was born, and a full 102 years before Luther nailed his Ninety-five Theses to the door of All Saint's Church in Wittenberg. Luther later referred to this prophecy by Hus. It's a rather remarkable story, and shows that one can persecute believers for their faith, but there is no way one can put an end to faith and to the dynamic church. There is, however, much more to Hus' story.

The followers of Hus were also persecuted and had to meet in secret for many years. The movement was almost eradicated from Czech lands and to make things worse, Hus' own followers fought among themselves and made some seriously flawed political moves. Finally, some from this persecuted group moved all the way to an estate in Saxony, in what today is Germany. These religious refugees had been invited to come to an area called Herrnhut to begin a new life. They were devout believers but not immune to conflict, extremism and to being manipulated by self-designed prophets. For a while it looked like even this group would vanish into irrelevancy.

Then something happened. Some of the leaders of this group called a meeting and actually persuaded the great majority of the members to forgive, agree with each other and to move forward. That meeting changed everything. The power of the Holy Spirit came into the room, the believers fell on their knees to pray and worship and the world witnessed how this group, also referred to as the Moravians, was changed into becoming one of the most strategic group of Christians since the early church.

As a result of this encounter, they decided to continue to pray. And they did that, 24/7 for one hundred years. They also began

1. Poggius The Papist, *Hus the Heretic*, Kessinger Publishing, LLC, March 10, 2003.

God and the Spiritual Tsunami

to go out as missionaries to some of the most needy areas of the world. Some sold themselves as slaves to be able to preach to slaves.

Their example opened the eyes of other Christians, and the movement for world missions has its roots in what happened at Herrnhut. Their faith and boldness influenced William Carey, the Baptist missionary pioneer from England, and the Danish king, Christian VI, to support a missionary endeavor. The Moravian Church is still a small denomination, but its influence has been enormous and is felt all over the world.

But it doesn't end there. John Wesley, the leader of the great Methodist revival in Britain, USA, and beyond, was heavily influenced by the Moravian movement. He first met a Moravian family on his way to what was to be a failed missionary effort in Georgia, USA. They were on the same ship and ran into a storm. Everyone on board feared for their life, except this family, who sat together, prayed and sang hymns. When asked how they could be so at peace during the storm, they answered: "We are not afraid to die." Wesley never forgot this. After his return to England he met one of the first Moravian bishops who was instrumental in helping John and his brother Charles see that it was faith in Christ, and not religious efforts, that offered assurance of salvation. A short time later they had the Aldersgate experience, when John Wesley experienced his heart becoming 'strangely warmed'. The program that evening was a Moravian leader reading the Introduction to Martin Luther's commentary to Galatians. It is not difficult to follow the lead here, is it? I think it is fair to call the resulting Wesleyan revival the precursor of the Holiness, Pentecostal and Charismatic movements that are sweeping the world today. There are definite similarities in spiritual experiences among them all.

There have, of course, been many other factors that have influenced this chain of events, but it is still a reminder that the old Tertullian saying about persecution is true. It did once look like the political and religious powers of Jan Hus' days had successfully stopped the spiritual renewal. But God saw to it that the world was going to hear, believe and be changed. They did roast 'the lean goose', but it came back through the swan and in many different forms with such power that it is the strongest force for global spiritual change that has ever been seen.

Jesus prepared His disciples for persecution. He was very clear and precise as to what it would entail. He even warned them that it would be wiser not to begin the journey of faith if they were not ready to face the potential consequences. It is a mystery how persecution, something so evil and wrong, can be such a force for good. The one explanation I like to remind myself about is that God will never, under any circumstances, let the suffering of Christians be just a useless and defeating thing. God will turn evil into good for the ones who trust in Him. That will not only happen in heaven, but already now, before heaven. That is one aspect of seeing how the growth of the Church and how it is persecuted are parallel occurrences. God can and will work through intricate and complex ways to fulfill His promises to believers. Sometimes it will even look like the persecuted Christians' lives ended in failure. But that is impossible, because God is absolutely true to His promises.

Jan Hus could not have foreseen how his life would one day influence world history. It is only in historical perspective that we can see that. It was the same situation when the apostle Paul was imprisoned. At the time, he might have looked weak, powerless and destitute, but after two thousand years, more people are influenced by his life and writings than ever before. That is an illustration of the mystery of persecution.

What would have happened if Jan Hus, (Global Revival) Thomas Cranmer (English Reformation) or Raymond Lull (converted by Jesus' revelations) had not followed their conscience, boldly preached Christ, and dared to die for their faith? Jan Hus and Thomas Cranmer were both burned at the stake, and in 1315 Raymond Lull, 80 years old at the time, was stoned for preaching Christ in Algeria (God is still using dreams and visions in the area where Lull was stoned to lead people to Jesus). Jesus foretold that His followers might be killed, but they would not be stopped.

Chapter 6

Follow the Signs: The Bible —A Reliable Record

In this chapter I aim to show that:

1. God has provided a way for us to learn about Him
2. He speaks through His prophets and acts in history according to what He has said
3. He gives us a reliable revelation of Himself through the Bible, which not only gives us important information but deeply influences the way we look at the world

THE BIBLE

I have always loved the Bible. One reason is that when I was a youth it was never suggested to me that the Bible was primarily a set of religious regulations. No, it contained true, real-life stories of how God spoke to His people through the prophets. It told us what God did and how He Himself became a man to show us who He really is—to save us from our own sins. He did that in a way that normal people can relate to, even though there is a wealth of information in the Biblical text that will take an eternity to really understand.

Follow the Signs: The Bible—A Reliable Record

The Bible is a collection of 66 books that describe how God reveals Himself to mankind. It tells us why we are in such a mess. It explains God's plan to save us from the consequences of sin. It demonstrates how Creation itself will display His glory and holiness forever. The Bible is a far more significant collection of books than the secular-minded are able to understand. It is the word of God.

No part of the Bible should be taken more lightly than another. The reason we honor the Old Testament is that Jesus called the Mosaic writings the word of God (Mark 7:9–13), and when we study His teachings, we see that He treated the entire Old Testament Canon that way. The New Testament books are regarded as authoritative because they were either written by an apostle who was directly commissioned by Jesus, or written during the apostolic era, that is, during a time when the leading eyewitnesses of Jesus' life and teaching , i.e the apostles, were still alive. There is a wealth of good books written about this, and some of them are listed at the end of this chapter. Here we are only going to look at why it is necessary to read the Bible regularly in order to understand its message and revelation.

Most of us have been tempted to read and enjoy only those portions of the Bible that relate to our own situation and be content to leave the rest for someone else to think about. This is not new; it has always been that way. Martin Luther was preoccupied with the question of justification by faith and did not feel that the Epistle of James helped him very much. He wrote that in his taste it was more straw than real food. One can understand this, because we, including even the great reformers, are mere humans and can't perceive all there is to be seen. As we read and experience the reality that the Bible leads us into, we need to be aware of our shortsightedness and try to read the Bible in a way that allows God to broaden our understanding rather than self-limit the revelation.

AN EXAMPLE FROM THE GENEALOGIES

The most common example of myopic reading of the Bible are the ways we often think about the Biblical genealogies—lists of names tracing the lines of descent. To the Western mind they don't seem necessary. To someone who was brought up in other parts of the world the genealogies might be some of the most powerful parts of the whole Bible. The reason is that the genealogies proclaim the faithfulness of God that is so often spoken about in the Biblical world: "And I will establish my covenant between me and you and your offspring after you throughout their generations for an everlasting covenant, to be God to you and to your offspring after you." (Genesis 17:7).

God promised Abraham a nation, and we have a whole list of persons from twelve different tribes reminding us that it really came to pass. There was the promise of a land, and that land had kings who go back to Abraham. The whole world was also going to be blessed, or bless themselves, because of Abraham. After 2000 years we see how Christ came as the fulfillment to bring that about. These genealogies remind us that we are part of something great that has been happening on the earth for 4000 years, and, according to Paul, followers of Christ are partakers of the blessing given to Abraham (Galatians 3:14).

The promises of God in the Bible are not just religious sayings given for our comfort. They do provide comfort, but that is because they remind us of God's promises that are grafted into the very history of which we are a part.

The genealogies do not only comfort us and remind us of God's promises; they also challenge us to reflect on our own lives. Not everyone who is mentioned in the genealogies believed and lived in a way that expressed faith in God. Some of the kings, for example, "did evil in the eyes of the Lord." They and people in their area of influence suffered because of that. There were periods when almost all of the people lived in rebellion to God. The nation of Israel was divided in two because of Solomon's sin. The kingdom of Israel was sent into captivity from which it never returned. The kingdom of Judah also went into captivity for 70 years. Having this great ancestry was not meant to be an excuse for idolatry and sin. Unconfessed sin always causes suffering. There are, however, two takeaways from this truth.

First, Daniel and a number of others found themselves as captives in Babylon and the successive empires as a result of the sins of others. They themselves, however, decided to learn from the disastrous consequences of sin and chose to live by faith in God. Daniel is actually described as one of the most righteous men in the history of the Bible, and is compared to Noah and Job (Ezekiel 14:14,20). Daniel and his friends were blessed by God and used by Him to bless and protect others.

The second takeaway is that God will always do what He has promised. Even those who oppose Him, like some of the persons in the Old Testament, will be instruments to bring about God's promises. They might be unwilling participants in this, but they will still be used by God, even if it is just to father children who will follow God, even though they might not accomplish anything of great significance themselves. The genealogies remind us that one day, on the very right day, people will see that God is absolutely trustworthy.

The mystery of how some unrighteous persons seem to be blessed gets a partial explanation in this. In the shorter perspective, it sometimes looks like evil and sin do not matter, and that dishonorable behavior can sometimes even be advantageous. Some of the worst persons in the Old Testament were kings for many years and were looked upon as the elite of society. But the judgment of history on these persons is fierce. They did what was evil and each one of them added guilt to the whole culture and led it into judgment.

The genealogies show us that it always pays off to be righteous in the long run, and often in the short run as well. They also show that someone will always have to pay for unrighteousness, sometimes right away and sometimes after a long period. The chase for immediate gratification is foreign to the world of the Bible. Abraham's faith and righteousness opened the way to receive the promised land after four hundred years. During the same four hundred years, the sins of some nations in the Middle East laid an unnoticed trap for them that led to their judgment.

Granted, we might not want to read the genealogies for our daily devotion every day of the week, but they do us a great service by reminding us of God's faithfulness to those who believe Him, and will protect us from giving up when the going is hard.

It is obvious that the Bible is not a modern Western book that was given to affirm our own peculiar way of living, be it right or wrong. Instead, it offers us a radically new way of understanding the world, and it is a way that works when we apply it thoughtfully to our everyday life. Reading the Bible consistently year after year will change our perspective of what is a successful life and what is not.

OUR BRAIN, OUR CULTURE AND THE BIBLE

The Bible introduces us to a new way of thinking and living. It actually leads us into a new cultural reality. One of the reasons why we think that our present and personal culture is the best is because culture molds the brain. With its incredible plasticity, it is ready to be imprinted by our culture and surroundings, making us take things for granted. This facilitates learning about human interaction in the part of the world where we grow up. On one level, the way our brains are influenced by our culture is therefore an immediate help. A less desirable consequence is that it often lures us to think that others are less cultured, less informed and more backward than we are.

Wars have been fought when one nation/culture bought into the lofty but chauvinistic goal of wanting to share its culture with its 'less fortunate' neighbors. This kind of thinking was one ingredient in defending the Napoleonic wars in Europe. The Russians often thought in a similar way as they invaded the Baltic nations. The Chinese have 'blessed' nearby people groups with their culture—a culture forced on them with military power. While this is tragic, one of the funniest illustrations of this cultural misconception was when the emissary from Pope Leo IX excommunicated some of the Greek Orthodox leaders in 1054. One of the less impressive arguments for the excommunication was that "they will not receive in communion those who tonsure their hair and shave their beards following the decreed practice of the Roman Church." In 1080 Pope Gregory VII forced the archbishop of Sardinia to shave his beard, "as the whole Western church have had the custom of shaving the beard from the very origins of the Christian faith." Ever heard of Jesus? Baptists, Charismatics, Republicans, Democrats, Canadians and Swedes are tempted to think the same manner. What we think of each other seems to us to be clear, rational and self-evident at the time, but when others look at us from a different perspective, it can look very petty.

This is one reason why people have such strong convictions of what is right and what is wrong. Some arguments are indeed petty, other questions are crucial, but there is no way of knowing what is right or wrong unless we have revelation from a perspective beyond our own. If humans are the final arbiters, then the post-modernists are right—any claim to 'truth' then leads to oppression and ultimately to post-truth societies. Yes, Paul does say that basic morals are naturally given, and Christians believe so, but the argument here is that there is no way to discern if something is morally right if there is no revelation. We must have a point of reference. We might know right from wrong in our hearts and be held responsible before God for our actions, but that is a different thing.

Now, it's important to clarify that the Biblical goal is not for there to be only one single, homogenous culture on earth. Just as the difference among individuals in any one culture enriches the whole, so it is with cultural variety between nations. The Biblical vision of the ultimate world is shown in the book of Revelation chapter 7:9–12.

> 9 After this I looked, and behold, a great multitude that no one could number, from every nation, from all tribes and peoples and languages, standing before the throne and before the

Lamb, clothed in white robes, with palm branches in their hands,

10 and crying out with a loud voice, "Salvation belongs to our God who sits on the throne, and to the Lamb!"

11 And all the angels were standing around the throne and around the elders and the four living creatures, and they fell on their faces before the throne and worshiped God,

12 saying, "Amen! Blessing and glory and wisdom and thanksgiving and honor and power and might be to our God forever and ever! Amen." (ESV)

The purpose for history is not uniformity; it is variety with one common purpose: to serve, honor and worship God. The variety of cultures enhances this eternal convivium.

There is only one way to grow into this. It is by actively letting our minds be renewed by revelation from God. There can be no other way, since all other known alternatives are just people convinced of their own understanding as the right and obvious one. The ones who, apart from Biblical revelation, try to introduce understanding and a generous view of others often end up trying to force their values on others. Now, moving in the direction of the Biblical vision is not easy, but it is necessary to do so if we are to serve others in the way God intends for us. It might be a good thing to read the Bible on our knees, like the late Archbishop William Temple did, asking for the guidance of the Holy Spirit.

HAVING THE BIBLE

We become Christians by believing in Jesus Christ. Maybe we should say it in an even clearer way: we do not become Christians through reading the Bible. The Early Church had no Bibles. That was also the case in the Western world during the Middle Ages. But there were Christians around, believing in Jesus Christ and doing their best to live the way they thought God called them to. The Christians who did not have the Bible would have had a much clearer understanding of who they were as believers if they had been able to read, learn and implement Biblical teaching. They would not have had as many misunderstandings, so much fear, superstitions and uncertainties if they had been exposed to the content of the Bible. We are saved by faith alone, but we grow as persons by seeing what God has revealed to us.

It is the greatest of privileges to have the Bible readily available, to be able to read, study, ponder, discuss and implement its teaching in our lives. It gives a clear understanding of who God is—His love, generosity, glory, holiness and unlimited power. It constantly reminds us of the high value that the Creator and Sustainer of the whole universe puts on us. It teaches us about the unfathomable love that was displayed by Christ, the Son of God, who is true God, when He died on the cross of Calvary for our sake. It teaches us how to live in a way that mirrors the character of God. And it gives us hope and great expectancy of what lies ahead after we die. When we take the Bible seriously it completely changes our lives.

READING THE BIBLE

When we read the Bible our outlook on life is changed. The apostle Paul defines it as a renewal of our minds. Paul says that as you read what he writes (Romans 12) and apply it to your life, your mind will not stay the same. It will be changed in a way that will help you to understand what God wants you to do in most circumstances.

Our very brains are changed by what we read, by what we hear, and by what we do. There is no middle or neutral ground. Our brains, and thereby our inner glasses that help us interpret the world around, are always in a process of change. They are influenced by our parents, authority figures, movies, news and daily experiences. We cannot and should not try to escape it. The good news is, however, that we are not slaves to our environment. We can filter our daily experiences through the revelation we have from God, and that will build a more mature, liberated way of

God and the Spiritual Tsunami

relating to the world around us. It will take time and discipline, but it does work wonders.

When we understand that the Bible is the Word of God, as Jesus calls it, we will begin to read it in an uncensored way. As long as we are uncertain of the Bible's status we will be tempted to read it with the restrictions that our culture wants us to have. Some people assert that miracles cannot have happened because they have not seen them in their own context. Certain New Testament moral standards should not be exercised because, it's argued, they are impossible, difficult or unfair to maintain. And certain teachings, like a need for the atonement, are not relevant to modern man. My response to those suggested restrictions on the Bible is: if it is true that God's promise to Abraham 4000 years ago is being actualized to this very day, that Jesus' promise to build His Church all over the earth is happening right before our eyes, and if the persecution that is meant to stop this Church actually becomes a means of intensifying its growth—well, then I'd be very hesitant to relativize the Bible. That is a very diplomatic way of saying that if we see God is faithful to His promises over thousands of years, then why would we doubt anything else He says? (Maybe the premises of what is called the Historic Critical Method are flawed, and should be exchanged for a more useful and accurate method in accordance with the reality we're seeing displayed around us. Just a thought.)

Being changed by the Word of God, the Bible, is a process. Since the goal of reading it is to learn truths formally, but also as importantly, to let ourselves be changed by its content, then it follows that it must take time. It will take years of daily reading. The worldview of the Bible is different from the one we have been brought up with in the Western world, and it takes time to see the inner side of another worldview. Reading the whole Bible, in a disciplined way year after year, will help us to see contexts, nuances, alternatives and realities from a newer perspective. It is enormously satisfying. It is in no way an irrational process. As a principle, anyone can experience this same inculturation by moving to a foreign culture for a long enough time. At first, we may be curious and positive to the new environment, then comes the culture shock and anti-reaction. Only after this, are we able to move 'into' the new culture and see it from the perspective of the native; by that time you will seem strange to the people you grew up with from your original culture because you will have changed. That is what happens when we are changed by God's word.

EVERYONE NEEDS TO GO THROUGH THIS PROCESS

The apostles of Christ needed to go through this process. They had just been taught by the greatest teacher in the history of mankind. The Biblical revelation is about Him, and they had the privilege of spending three years with Him. One would think that they would have had it all together by then. But that was not the case.

When Jesus taught them about the reason He had come to earth—to be rejected, crucified and then resurrected after three days—they did not understand what He was talking about.

- 31 And taking the twelve, he said to them, "See, we are going up to Jerusalem, and everything that is written about the Son of Man by the prophets will be accomplished.
- 32 For he will be delivered over to the Gentiles and will be mocked and shamefully treated and spit upon.
- 33 And after flogging him, they will kill him, and on the third day he will rise."
- 34 But they understood none of these things. This saying was hidden from them, and they did not grasp what was said. (Luke 18:31–34 ESV)

When they heard the reports about the resurrection they thought it was "idle tale, and they did not believe them" (Luke 24:11 ESV).

They needed to meet the resurrected Jesus in order to understand that the promises in the Bible were real and not figurative truth.

God and the Spiritual Tsunami

Later, in the book of Acts, they had been convinced about the resurrection, and had received the Holy Spirit that Jesus had promised them. They preached and thousands were converted, the sick were healed, they had been let out of prison by an angel and even raised a lady named Dorcas from the dead—but they needed clear guidance from the Holy Spirit to see that the Gospel was meant to be preached to all nations, not only to the Jews. It took some time to arrive at that revelation, which is described in Acts 10—11. Not only did Peter need clear instructions from heaven to begin to preach to the Gentiles, but after he did so he had to defend himself to the church leadership. There are no negative comments about Peter and the church leadership in the story. It seems like Luke, the author of Acts, looks upon this learning process as something quite normal. But here is the bottom line: if the apostles needed time, prayer and the guidance from God to do what they later understood had been in the Scriptures all the time, and they had been taught by Jesus, it is more than highly probable that we all need time for the message of the Bible to sink in. It would be foolish to think that we have it all together, when the apostles did not. This is an understatement.

The apostles learned to understand God's purposes as they are revealed in the Bible by prioritizing the reading and teaching of the Bible, by spending time with God in prayer, by doing what they were told in the Bible, and being a part of the Christian community called the Church.

This is the way we learn to understand the heart of the Bible and the way in which we allow our minds to be changed by its message.

It is necessary to have this attitude to the Bible if we want to get its real message. On the other hand, having this attitude does not mean that we will understand everything. Far from it. One of the first things we learn is that there is a huge difference between knowing the revealed truth about someone or something and having a lot of information. As soon as we understand what it means to live under the perspective of revealed truth, we will discover the limits of our understanding and be quick to acknowledge it.

Follow the Signs: The Bible—A Reliable Record

As in the case of one's salvation: it is possible to be absolutely certain that our sins are forgiven and that we are fully justified by faith in Jesus Christ without fully understanding how God worked that out. We know what we know because God has revealed it to us in the Bible and we trust it. This is what faith is all about.

Chapter 7

The Tsunami and What to Expect: Change

The Continued Global Growth of the Church In this chapter I aim to show that:

1. The growth of the global church has just begun
2. God Himself leads this process sovereignly
3. There will be both a great variety and great unity in this movement

CHANGE

Be prepared for change. The Church will continue to grow. It will probably not look the way we expect in the West. It will be much more spontaneous, dynamic, true to the original Biblical concept of the Church. At the same time, there will be a great, and maybe confusing, variety of expressions.

When Jesus told the first generation believers to make all nations into His disciples, they might have had a hint of what that could mean, but the Book of Acts shows us that they had no clue how to make it happen. They certainly did not have control of the development, but were fully dependent on the power, guidance and wisdom of the Holy Spirit. As soon as they thought that they

The Tsunami and What to Expect: Change

knew how to lead the Church they were redirected by the Spirit in the direction they needed to take, but that they had not seen, even though it had been foretold in the Scriptures for hundreds of years. There is not even a whiff of criticism of this in the Bible. It just states the facts about how God Himself led the development and the extension of the Church. It just had to be that way; that is also the way it is to this very day. There are a lot of negative comments about the fact that not only churches multiply but it is also denominations. Some scholars claim that there are more than fifty thousand denominations in the world. Some of these are sectarian, some have been born from disagreements and selfishness, and some out of sheer stupidity. But the vast majority are made up of truly Christian groups of believers. They have been born out of necessity in situations that can be understood only as we meet and listen to the persons involved.

Let me take one example from China. We met with a leader for one of the 'smaller' house church movements. They numbered about 1.2 million a few years ago. By now they might have doubled. Their leader was converted after he had been killed in a workplace related accident, and an aunt of his prayed for his healing because she knew he needed to believe in Jesus to be saved. She obviously got her request answered, and our friend woke up and discovered that he had been healed. It did not take much more convincing to become a Christian. He then began to share his faith, many others received Christ, and it spread. At the same time, the new movement had to be kept underground to evade the searches of the police, so it took a long time before they met other Christian leaders. One day he happened to meet an Anglican minister or bishop, he did not know the formal title, but as they shared their faith and discovered that they were one in all the basics of the faith, the Anglican ordained this Chinese leader. He told us with a smile that he had been ordained by a minister of Her Majesty's Church. I don't know if this revelation just added a few million adherents to its membership. Probably not. When we met, our friend had not been able to visit his own home for two years, because the police

God and the Spiritual Tsunami

were searching for him. That was the beginning of one of these denominations.

Another leader of an unregistered house church movement told me that they organized themselves as house churches, not out of theological or sociological reasons, but because it was the only way they could practically do it at this time. They might change format in the future if necessary.

There is a beautiful aspect of this. No organization, office or hierarchy has control over it. Much of it, probably most of it, happens spontaneously in response to practicalities. But there is of course a plan behind it—that plan is designed by God Himself. It might just look disorganized and not at all strategic from a Western perspective. But we would make a huge mistake if we see what happens in the Church from a mere Western perspective. We Westerners love simple order: what seems like strategic planning and five-year plans. On one level that is a good thing. We do need to take responsibility to organize what God entrusts to us so that it will thrive and express God's intentions. It is, however, important to understand the scope of our responsibility as humans under God. We should take responsibility for what God has entrusted to us and then dare to trust that God knows what He is doing when He does what He wants in other situations. What looks unorganized might just be a spiritual organism being developed in a way that looks surprising to us. Whatever we think of this, the phenomenal growth of the believing church will continue and nothing, not even the decision centers of Hell can withstand it.

God can and does use a combination of Biblical guidance in a way that blows our minds. Reading the story of the birth of Jesus illustrates this:

1. A priest named Zechariah was chosen by lot to minister in the Temple of Jerusalem. If he was chosen, this honor would be his for only one time in his life. From a secular perspective this looks like a chance event.

2. The angel Gabriel from God appeared and announced a to Zechariah that he and his wife would get a son who would be

The Tsunami and What to Expect: Change

the forerunner to the coming of the Lord (Luke 1:8-17. This was to fulfill a prophecy in Malachi 4:5.

3. A while later, the angel Gabriel appeared to a young girl, Mary, and announced that she is going to be pregnant through a miracle from God and be the mother of the much longed for Messiah. (Luke 1:26-38 compared to Isaiah 7-9)

4. Joseph, Mary's future husband, was visited by an angel who told him that Mary was pregnant through a miracle from God. He was told to name the boy to be born 'Jesus'. All of it happened to fulfill a 700-hundred year-old prophecy from Isaiah about a virgin who would conceive the future Messiah. (Matt 1:18-23)

5. The Emperor in Rome decided to register everyone in the Roman Empire. This seems to be one of the many whims of Emperors and kings, and does certainly not look like it is meant to fulfill ancient Messianic prophecies. However, this forced Joseph and Mary to go to Bethlehem, their ancestral city, even though it must have seemed irrational since Mary was pregnant, and the most comfortable means of travel for a poor family was to ride a donkey.

6. After Jesus was born "wise men from the east" came to worship him bringing gifts. There are lots of suggestions as to what these wise men were, from where they came and what the star really was. I have some thoughts about that myself but this is not the place to argue for them. We really don't know much about this. The story does tell us though that the signs of the newly born Messiah were so clear that anyone open to look for them would have no difficulty to see them and act appropriately. (Matt 2:1-6)

7. The Biblical experts of the day, the scribes, affirmed that the Messiah would be born in Bethlehem, and they based their information on an Old Testament prophecy that was readily available. (Matt 2: 3-6)

8. The wise men were warned by an angel not to go back to king Herod but to depart directly to their own country. (Matt 2:12)

9. Herod, the paranoid local king, felt threatened by the information from the wise men and the scribes informing him that the Messiah had been born, so he decided to kill all male children in the Bethlehem area. (Matt 2:16-18)

10. An angel ordered Joseph to flee to Egypt away from Herod's rage, which also fulfills another Old Testament prophecy. (Matt 2:13-15)

11. After Herod died an angel ordered Joseph to bring his family back to Israel. (Matt 2:19-21)

12. When Joseph heard that the province of Judea was ruled by Herod's son, Archelaus, he was afraid to go there. (Matt 2:22a)

13. Joseph then had a dream and was told to move to Galilee. (Matt 2:22b)

14. As they came to Galilee Joseph decided to settle in the city of Nazareth, which also came to fulfill an Old Testament prophecy that said that the child would be called a Nazarene. Nazareth was located in Galilee. (Isaiah 9:1)

15. At some point Joseph and Mary brought Jesus to the Temple of Jerusalem to offer the sacrifice of the poorer families in gratitude for the child. The sacrifice was probably also understood as a dedication of the child to the purposes of God. At this time, two older persons, Simeon and Hannah, appeared on the scene independently of each other, but prophetically led by the Holy Spirit. They sought out the child and thanked God for fulfilling His promise to the people of Israel.

These are 15 different cases of God's leading assuring that His plan for the salvation of the world would be started in the right way. But the guidance cannot be seen as a simple straight line. There were angels announcing and directing, plus some prophetic persons, and we probably expect that in some way. But there is also the pagan emperor Augustus making a administrative decision

The Tsunami and What to Expect: Change

that does not seem to have anything to do with the fulfillment of Old Testament prophecy. The Emperor had no idea of these implications of his actions, and had he known, he might even have tried to prevent the whole thing. One day it would mean the end of the Roman Empire.

Then there are the wise men; we don't know how many they were, from which country or religion. All we know is that they, in contrast to the 'specialists', knew that the Messiah had been born. Finally, Joseph's fear triggered the dream that led them to Judea while the Gospel text just gives us the impression that he thought Nazareth would be a good place to live.

In all of this, God saw to it that His plan would be fulfilled. In contrast, the self- described specialists, the Scribes, could know and did know, but did not act or even react to the information available. They, the king, and the people in Jerusalem were struck by fear instead of responding to hope.

This was not a one-time thing. This amazing variety and integration of direction, circumstances and action abounds throughout the Christian narrative. For example, the Book of Acts gives us a similar story about the miraculous birth of the Church at Pentecost and its development.

The lesson from the very first beginning of the Christian faith is that believers had better take God's way of communicating and guiding into account. It will look very different from our own expectations, not because faith in God is weird, but because we don't have enough information to judge the Divine interventions correctly.

It is a little bit like when quantum physics was discovered. It took some time until the scientific community accepted it, and the greatest physicist of them all, Einstein, struggled with the concept most of his life. Mankind is still learning to live with the fact that something may look counter-intuitive but still be true. We are in the process of struggling to follow the rational evidence rather than our desire for intuitive rationality. Similarly, we also have to learn to listen to God and His revelation and adjust our opinions and life accordingly. We have been shown beyond a shadow of a doubt that God works in history. Most often He does that in ways that are unpredictable. But since He told beforehand that He would intervene in history to accomplish His purposes, it is rational, prudent and morally necessary to take what He has foretold into account. The way He will accomplish what He said will come as a surprise, but it will happen in a way that anyone who is open will recognize and understand.

THE BEGINNING OF THE CHURCH

We have already looked at what happened on the day of Pentecost and what a surprise that was for everyone, both believers and opposition. But that was only the beginning. The first church and its leaders needed God's clear direction at all important new steps they needed to take.

The Apostles needed a life-long learning process of how to understand the Scriptures. They were aware of how God had led history and the individual lives of each person. They had seen the revelation of Jesus Christ, that we read about, and experienced how their lives were used to fulfill Old Testament prophecies. Now they were the leaders.

The Apostles knew the Scriptures and saw them as the highest authority for seeing truth. Their Scriptures were what we today call the Old Testament or Tanakh, and were the recognized collection of the prophetic revelation from the writings of Moses through Second Chronicles ('Malachi' in the Church tradition). They believed and taught that these prophetically given writings were ultimately given by God and were to be trusted and obeyed fully by anyone who wanted to profess faith in the God of Israel.

The Apostles were, of course, influenced by what Jesus had taught them by words and personal commitment. Jesus did not only teach verbally that the words of the Bible were the very words of the Father. He showed how deeply He trusted the Father's promises through the prophets, by walking to Jerusalem in order to be crucified and then resurrected on the third day. That is the way the Apostles continued to teach and to live. We need to understand

and emulate this depth of dedication in order to live with the same dynamic relationship to God as the Apostles did.

A HIGH VIEW OF THE SCRIPTURES CHALLENGED THE APOSTLES TO CONSTANTLY DISCOVER THEIR MEANING

The Apostles were soon to discover that believing the Bible and knowing the words is one thing. It is often quite another thing to understand what God actually is saying. The Apostles had a high view of the Scriptures, but they had to learn to understand their meaning the way God had intended. They sometimes interpreted Scripture in the same culturally tainted way their contemporaries did. The problem with that, of course, is that all groups of people have a tendency to adjust their interpretation of the Bible in a way that supports their own preferred way of living and excuses their criticism of others whom they perceive to be wrong.

Jesus had to explain the real meaning of the Scriptures to the disciples time and time again. The Pharisees thought that the Scriptures were on their side, so did the Sadducees; in fact, Jesus' own disciples were convinced that their understanding of the Bible was the ultimate one. That the disciples thought so makes perfect sense, since they were taught by Jesus and even did the same kind of signs and wonders that He did. But Jesus showed them that they still had to learn. Even after Pentecost, when they were the leaders of the church, they had to rethink and learn under the guidance of the Holy Spirit.

The same is true today. We tend to understand the Bible the way our own group understands it. It is only as we are forced by God Himself to listen and have our eyes opened that we begin to really understand and live the Bible. That leads us to see that we need the community of believers to understand, but we also need personal reflection on the Bible as well as personal illumination by the Holy Spirit.

It is important to remember that Jesus did not introduce them to a deeper meaning of the Scriptures, but helped them to understand what was really there all the time, and for everyone to see.

Take Paul as an example. He read the same Scriptures after his conversion as he did before, but there was a big difference. Before his encounter with the risen Jesus Christ he used his understanding of the Scriptures to kill Christians. Afterwards he argued from the same Scriptures as he tried to lead Jewish leaders to belief in Jesus Christ. He needed to meet the reality of the Bible in order to begin to understand it.

A MULTIFACETED APPROACH

The Apostles began to understand the real meaning of what the Scriptures said when they saw the power of God revealed through Jesus, as the Holy Spirit led them, as God's power worked through their own lives, and as they grew in understanding by following God's instructions. This multifaceted process is clearly seen in the further examples of how Peter was called to preach to the Gentiles, how Paul and Silas were sent out, and how the Apostolic meeting about circumcision came to change the course of history.

We know how Peter was called to preach to Cornelius, the Gentile officer. As a believing Jew, Peter knew the content of the Bible as well as anyone else. He was the point leader of the church and had been trained by Jesus Christ Himself. But Peter still did not get it. He needed a personal challenge from God Himself to prepare him to preach to this spiritually hungry man, who had been seeking God for years. And it was not only Peter! The believing, and quite adventurous Jewish men who went with him were astonished when they saw that the Holy Spirit filled Cornelius and his friends when they believed. And there is more—Peter had to defend his actions to the other leaders in the church. He had done something that no one had done before, and which the leader was not expected to do: to visit the home of a Gentile and eat with him. Only when Peter, and later the church leaders, saw what God Himself had done did they understand that this was what God had previously said through the Old Testament prophets. They did not

The Tsunami and What to Expect: Change

introduce a new theology or stretch the meaning of the Biblical text to fit what they thought it ought to mean, as often has been done in the church. They just discovered what God had led them to understand and actually do precisely as God had promised centuries earlier.

Many of the Christians in Peter's time did not get it. They were wonderful believers who paid a high price of persecution for their commitment to Jesus. They were willing to be driven from their homes for the love for Jesus, but even after Peter's experience they only preached the Gospel to their own people, the Jews. This went on for some time. An exception was some remarkable believers in Antioch, "who on coming to Antioch spoke to the Hellenists also, preaching the Lord Jesus." (Acts 11:20) They had integrated what they had discovered from the Scriptures into their lives and were preparing the entire church for the Holy Spirit's next important step.

In Acts chapter 20 we are told that the Holy Spirit prophetically told the church leadership in Antioch that it was to release Paul and Silas for the work that he had called them to do. This clearly was not the result of the Church's long term plan, but was a direct, new initiative by the Holy Spirit. This church, which had already begun to take the important steps of obedience by preaching to the Gentiles, became the strategic center for world missions. Their hearts and minds were prepared and they were in the habit of obeying the Scriptures. The rest is history.

Paul and Silas continued to preach in the Jewish synagogues, because they were convinced that the Jewish community should have the privilege of hearing the Gospel first, but as soon as they felt it was the right time, they preached to everyone who wanted to hear, regardless of nationality.

There remained, however, uncertainty by others in the church as to its proper mission and method for reaching the Gentiles. In Acts chapter 15 we are told that some Christians from Judea, where the Church was born, claimed that since it was clear that the Gentiles could be included in God's church, they needed first to become circumcised, which was meant to indicate that they were first to become Jews. Being a Jew was looked upon as an honor by the first church, but they understood clearly that it was not necessary for salvation. The Apostles and the elders of the Jerusalem church met and decided, however, that since God had already given the Holy Spirit to the Gentiles who believed, and since the Scriptures said that both Jews and Gentiles were going to be included in the church, no one had the right to demand circumcision for believing Gentiles.

> "'After this I will return,
> and I will rebuild the tent of David that has fallen;
> I will rebuild its ruins,
> and I will restore it,
>
> that the remnant of mankind may seek the Lord,
> and all the Gentiles who are called by my name,
> says the Lord, who makes these things known from of old.'" (Acts 15:16–18)

The argument made was from Scripture, and was understood as they compared the prophets' words to God's clear intervention in the life of the church.

The way the Apostles learned to understand the Scriptures was by reading them, obeying them, seeing God at work according to them, and by the illumination of the Spirit. The Apostles would never dream of adding to the Scriptures, questioning them or contradicting them. They were so committed to their authority that they, like Jesus, were willing to do anything to live according to them and to experience the life that God promises those who believe and obey Him.

What happens in the global Church today is a powerful reminder of the dynamics of what went on in the first century Church. We should look at what God did in the beginning to be prepared for what is going to happen during our own era of history, when the expansion of Jesus' Church has taken off in a new and dramatic way.

WHAT WE CAN EXPECT

The expansion of the Church will continue and increase to a degree that Jesus' mandate in Matthew 28 will be fulfilled. Please hear me out. There is no Western Christendom triumphalism in saying this. The West has very little to do with it. Most of what happens is the result of God working independently of human or even ecclesiastical agencies. What is done from Western churches is done in response to God's calling to share the Gospel and minister to the poor. That is obviously a right way of living as Christ-followers. However, and this is important, the expansion of the Church has very little to do with these efforts. All it does is illustrate that God is always working on a multiple number of levels to accomplish His purposes.

The goal of salvation history is to make all nations disciples to Jesus. That is not just His desire; it is what He is about to do. Before He told his disciples to make disciples of all nations, He reminded them that He has all power in heaven and on earth. He also reminded them (Gospel of Luke chapter 21) that the Scriptures had prophesied that the Messiah would suffer and be raised on the third day, and (!) that the Gospel would be preached among all nations. If we believe that Jesus really is the Son of God we should expect this to happen. We don't have the time schedule for it, and as with many things that God has promised, it will sometimes look like the effort has failed. It certainly looked like that when Jesus hung on the cross. Today, we see an unprecedented movement to Christ which should challenge us to look deeper in the Scriptures and history. It will, for one thing, remind us that God is doing today exactly what He promised so long ago.

When Jesus said that all nations will become disciples He obviously did not mean that 100% of the earth's population would become believers. He Himself told us that there will come a final judgment when some are welcomed into heaven while others will be sent to eternal judgment, away from God. Instead, it means that so many will believe that one can refer to a nation now as a nation of Jesus' followers. Whether that means 20 or 80% we don't know, but we currently are seeing the beginning of something extraordinary happening before our eyes.

This expansion is taking place on all continents except in parts of Europe. The world has never seen anything like it before. It also happens in countries where the Church is under extreme pressure from governments and or local cultures. No person or organization can claim responsibility for the growth. It is most assuredly a Divine initiative, much like the description we read about in the book of Acts.

WHAT WILL IT LOOK LIKE?

Faithfulness to the original Christian message

Much of the growth and renewal of the Church takes place in hostile environments, or in areas where there are such great needs that mere words, good as they might be, are not enough. In those situations, a secular religiosity does not get a hearing. People who risk their reputation, and sometimes their own lives, want to know if what they adopt is really true. To suffer for their faith, they have to believe that the Bible is totally true and trustworthy. They believe that everything in the Apostle's Creed means exactly what the early church meant. An old friend who had spent many years in Communist prison for his faith said that there were no "liberals" in the prison, and by the way, no one cared which denomination a person belonged to. The growing, dynamic Church is a bulwark against reductionistic theology and will stay that way.

LEADERSHIP GIVEN BY THE HOLY SPIRIT

In almost all human institutions there is both a formal as well as a real, dynamic leadership. Sometimes the two are intertwined, but not always. People tend to give lip service to formal leadership, but actually listen more to, and follow more readily, real dynamic leadership. It does not take long to discover who the real leaders are in an organization, and how irritating those leaders are to persons

The Tsunami and What to Expect: Change

in a formal but not effective role. This was the case in the first Church. The formal religious leadership was appalled that people would follow "unlearned men" from a northern province, and not the intellectual and religious institutions in Jerusalem. Basically all renewal movements in the Church since then have met the same rejection. Some of the fastest growing churches in the USA are led by pastors who have no or little theological education, and some of the more traditionalist critics have not hesitated to point that out. Meanwhile, the trend continues all over the world. God uses both well trained theologians and not so well trained leaders, because He sees to the heart. He uses the same standard as when He chose David to be king, to the surprise of His own prophet, Samuel.

In history, He chose the Apostle Peter, a former fisherman, whose New Testament Greek was not the usual. His ministry was, however, approved by God who acted with signs and wonders as Peter proclaimed the Gospel. He showed a similar approval of Bishop Athanasius of Alexandria who stood for the historic Christian message at a time when almost the whole church, with support of the Emperor, opposed him. He used the mathematical genius Pascal and the self-taught preacher Charles Haddon Spurgeon, Billy Graham with a college degree, and Dwight Moody who just had a very basic education and who struggled with English grammar. Their intellect was impressive, their commitment total, their dependence on the power of the Holy Spirit very clear, and their influence enormous.

Today the very same reality is seen all over the world. The fastest growing church in Sweden, Stockholm Hillsong (and it is growing fast), is led by a young pastor who clearly is led by the Holy Spirit and has a noticeable gift of leadership, and evangelism, but had only a rudimentary theological education when the church started. One just needs to visit the church, and take a good look into its life, to see that it is clearly blessed by God to reach large numbers of unchurched young people. All this is in one of the world's most secular countries.

On the other hand, our home church, The Woodlands Church, one of the fastest growing churches in USA, is led by a pastor who was trained at one of the best theological seminaries in the country. He is theologically very astute and is a brilliant communicator, but knows that he is totally dependent on the Holy Spirit for the church to flourish and be a healthy, attractive and blessed place for unchurched people to find new life in Christ. Texas is one of the most spiritually open cultures in the West.

One of the churches with most impact in London, England, is an Anglican church, Holy Trinity Brompton (HTB), where thousands have come to faith in Christ. They minister to 4000 visitors every week, have re-planted more than 20 churches in the region, and started the Alpha Course that has reached millions and blessed churches from a multitude of denominations. Its ministry was so significant that the Anglican Archbishop of Kampala, with the blessing of the diocese of London, made the former vicar of HTB a bishop. The present vicar, Nicky Gumbel, former lawyer turned priest, developed the Alpha Course to what has now become one of the world's best known evangelistic tools.

There are hundreds of thousands of other national leaders all over the world who fit the vast spectrum of gifts, personality and style. Their theology varies from one to another: some are staunch evangelicals, some charismatic, some are from house churches, some from liturgical, ancient churches, and some are very hard to define. But the mosaic looks quite a lot like the picture we see in the book of Acts and in the early Church. We must get used to this, because it seems to be the way God works in His Church all over the world.

There are, of course, off-shoots of this dynamic church that have moved outside the parameters of what it means to be a Christian church. It has always been that way. The Apostles had to deal with it, and throughout history wicked alternatives to the Church have always surfaced. According to Paul this might even be necessary, in order to demonstrate which professing believers stay true to the Gospel of Christ and which don't. The off-shoots have been called Gnostics, Montanists, Arian or have gone undercover in the larger churches. During Bishop Athanasius' tenure it seemed that the larger part of the church was following a heretic named Arius.

The Tsunami and What to Expect: Change

Athanasius' struggle has been described as one man standing up against the rest of the world: Athanasius Contra Mundum. This is played out today within some of the theological extreme movements. It might come as a surprise to us as Westerners to realize that some of our own historical churches have departed so far from the given faith that they are no longer recognized as legitimate churches by the leading older churches in the two-thirds world.

One of the largest and most dynamic churches in the Middle East is located on the Hill of the Mokattam and is led by a Coptic priest. In 1969, the governor of Cairo decreed that all those employed as trash removers, who were largely Coptic Christians, could only live at the Hill of the Mokattam. These Christians are among the poorest of the poor in Egypt and have suffered harassment for their faith for generations. One of the residents of Mokattam invited a Coptic priest to relocate and minister to the local population of 15,000. At first the priest resisted. After time, and a strong prompt from the Holy Spirit, he relented and decided to visit. Unannounced he took a bus to the area and was surprised to find the very man who had invited him waiting for him at the bus stop. The trash remover had been informed of his impending visit by the Holy Spirit.

He was overwhelmed at what he saw of poverty and ignorance and decided to stay and ask God for direction. He did so on the top of the waste mountain that the collectors had gathered over the years. One day a wind blew a piece of paper to his location and when he looked at it he saw that it was a page from a discarded Bible. On the page he read: "The Lord spoke to Paul in a vision: 'Do not be afraid; keep on speaking, do not be silent. For I am with you, and no-one is going to attack and harm you, because I have many people in this city.'" (Acts 18:9, 10) He saw this as a confirmation from God that he was supposed to minister to these people. Later they found a cave that was turned into a large church that today gathers thousands for services. The church does not at all fit any Western definition: it is Coptic, rather Evangelical, and definitely Charismatic. If you want to get a feel for what it is like, take a look at a video from a prayer service a few years ago where you will see thousands of Egyptians chant "Jesus" for ten minutes in a row.

One of the lessons from this overview is that any attempt to use old, extra-Biblical criteria to understand the kind of leadership that emerges will fail. So also will attempts to organize the dynamic, growing Church into a human institutional unity. The kind of Church we are describing already lives in unity with other believers, denominations and congregations that proclaim the given, apostolic message. And the world believes!

DYNAMIC CHURCHES

The global movement of growing churches is dynamic. Their leaders and members believe and act in a way that shows that the reality of the New Testament is meant to be the experience of all Christians. They do, of course, represent a number of theological varieties as how to understand and communicate this, but there is a basic agreement that the reality is there.

It is hard to visit most churches in Africa and at the same time deny the reliability of the Bible, or to believe that miracles do not happen after a certain time in the early Church. A good friend of mine had to change his theology drastically after coming to Ethiopia as a professor of Theology. He came as an excellent Evangelical theologian, but when he saw the life and dynamics in one of the fastest growing Lutheran churches he also understood that his Western, professed Evangelical theology had been colored by Western rationalism and lack of authentic Biblical experience. The experience of real healing miracles and real freedom from psychological and physical oppression tends to create a new understanding of God's Biblical intentions and power today.

It is natural and necessary to discuss the theology behind this dynamic. Is it because some people use their spiritual gifts, or does it happen because Christians pray? That kind of discussion ought to be held within an open and authentic community. The world of the dynamic, growing Church needs and keeps healthy by those kinds of conversation. But the backdrop needs to be the reality of

The Tsunami and What to Expect: Change

God's intervention in the daily life of His Church. It is too overwhelming to deny.

What we see in today's growing church has been a part of the Church through the ages, when it has been healthy. In the 300s Athanasius recounted how God prepared him prophetically for coming threats; so much so that his heretical opponents accused him of sorcery. A century later, Augustine described a number of miracles of healing in his book "Retractions." Martin Luther was healed after his co-worker Philip Melanchthon pleaded with God for his life. The Pietist leader August Hermann Francke built an orphanage without appealing to anyone for funds. God consistently provided the necessary resources through touching the hearts of Christians in response to Francke's prayers.

Excesses and plain fraud in the two-thirds world and in the West have made many weary of these phenomena, and so it should be. However, we need to watch out so we don't throw the baby out with the bathwater.

VARIETY

One cannot help but be struck by seeing the incredible variety of church style that God seems to bless. In South Korea, it seems to be the Presbyterian churches that have the greatest response. In Taiwan, it is often liturgical churches; in South America it is Pentecostal and Charismatic groups. In Africa, it is all of the above.

An illustration of this variety is an open letter from some of the leading Chinese churches to the Communist government where they assure the government of their loyalty to each other in spite of their theological differences and variety of style. They very clearly state that they respect each other and recognize each other as expressions of the Church.

In China, because of the less than intelligent reaction from the government, many of the growing churches are forced to organize as house churches. In some Muslim dominated countries believers cannot meet in groups larger than five or six. They are shunned by the community, distrusted by the few existing churches that are around and they are sought by the secret police.

A priest from the Coptic church in Egypt has had an enormous influence in the Arab world, and in 2011 more than 70,000 Coptic Christians gathered at the Cave Church outside Cairo for an evening of prayer and worship. It looked like an enormous Hillsong event.

This also happens in the West. Churches like Willow Creek Community Church and The Woodlands Church have left some of the traditional ways of doing church in order to reach the unchurched, and they have surely met a need. The American Sociologist Rodney Stark researched this and found that attendants in most of these newer churches had a deeper faith, read their Bible more often, prayed more, and shared their faith more than the average attendant in older, smaller churches.

This ever-increasing variety illustrates the saying that it is probably better to stay true to the message and be open to organizational and cultural change in the Church than to do the opposite: keep the form but change the message.

SOCIAL RESPONSIBILITY

Most of the Biblically based, growing churches have a realistic view of history. They understand that no group—Christian, religious or secular—will be able to solve all the problems in the world. Their reasoning is that even though we know every individual will die one day it is our duty and privilege to live as responsibly we can, to take care of our bodies, save for the future and to see a physician when our bodies malfunction. We are created in the image of God, and we should take that seriously. It is the same with creation and society. Yes, there will be problems, wars, natural disasters and sickness, but even though we cannot change the whole world we need to express our identity as Christ-followers and create as many local expressions of the Kingdom of God as possible. That has been the trademark of the Church through all centuries, and it is so to this very day.

The Tsunami and What to Expect: Change

Few people know that organizations like the League of Nations (the forerunner of the United Nations) and the Red Cross were started by persons who had been impacted by Christian revivals. The Methodist revival in England brought not only a renewal to many churches but influenced the government to make education available to all children, regardless of socio-economic background. It also improved conditions for the poor farm-workers and factory-workers. Some historians believe that the Methodist revival saved England from the horrors that the French revolution brought on to itself neighboring country.

When the one-child policy was still in effect, Christians in China often adopted children from families that had more than one child. They did this to their own peril and paid a high cost. One denomination that is mainly active in the countryside has a vision that its members live on just ten percent of their income and give 90% to provide for the destitute.

The Anglican church in Kenya is actively involved in a program called "Just Earth" to help poor farmers all over the country to increase their crops by learning long-term, sustainable methods of farming. One of the most powerful organizations within that church is the Mothers' Union (from the Anglican Church) which not only works to help women who are vulnerable in an unstable environment, but also provides weekly nourishing meals to hundreds of thousands of orphans who are victims of the AIDS epidemic.

This ethos for social responsibility will always be a sign of authentic church life. It has been, is, and will be criticized by organized religious groups and by secular institutions because it communicates more of the love of Christ than mere words and requires more than lip service. Social responsibility in this context is not missions or evangelism, like many secularized churches in the West define those terms. But even when it is distinguished from missions it brings with itself a powerful message that shows one significant aspect of Christian life.

God and the Spiritual Tsunami

PROJECTIONS FOR THE FUTURE

If the present trend continues, and it will, there will soon be more Evangelical Christians in China than in the United States. There will also be a majority of Christians in Indonesia within 20 years. This explains why resistance from radical Islamists is growing in that country.

Interestingly, the number of committed Christ-followers in the United States might actually be growing. It is very difficult to prove this statistically today, but there are indications that as the older, secularized denominations decline, along with most of the culture-conservative groups, there is a fresh movement of new, dynamic churches emerging. They have more in common with their brothers in China, Africa and South America than traditional churches in their home city.

More people have come to Christ since 1950 than in the whole previous history of the Church. It comes as a surprise both to the secular interpreters of the contemporary world and to most Christians in the West. A North American pastor, John Piper, has noted that the global Church is growing so quickly today that the majority of Christ-followers do not know English and have never said a word in English. It is a fascinating time to be a Christian.

Chapter 8

The Tsunami and What to Expect: Revival in the Muslim World

In this chapter I aim to show that:

1. There will continue to be a powerful movement towards Jesus Christ in the Muslim world
2. God is sovereignly in charge of this movement
3. We can expect much blessing but also strong opposition to this

THE END OF ISLAM AS A POLITICAL POWER

Saudi Arabia has historically been one of the most dictatorial nations in the world, not unlike North Korea and Brunei in its wrath against dissenters. Anyone who denounces Islam is severely punished, often by beheading, and citizenship is only awarded to those who are Muslim. So imagine a day when 20% of its population has become Christian (20% is a conservative estimate). This country will one day be unrecognizable. In fact, the process of many turning to Jesus Christ has already begun, and once it has begun there is no way to stop it.

God and the Spiritual Tsunami

Another example, which has moved from the unimaginable to the now happening, is Iran. It is another dictatorial state, led into an acceptance of extremism through the Ayatollah Khomeini. He and the Shia leadership in the country of the day would have had no idea that what they got started would be the beginning of the end of Islamic dominance in their country.

How can we be so sure this will take place? Let me assure you that the argument has absolutely nothing to do with Western supremacy, but has everything to do with what God has promised and what He clearly is doing today in bringing nations to Himself.

First, a reminder of the premise of this book: God always does what He has promised. God's covenants and promises are irrevocable. Not because God could not change His mind. He could, and there are instances in the Biblical narrative where God says that He intends to judge a nation but then changes His mind as a response to the prayer of a believer. Those events are reported on a human/ micro level. But they never intended to imply that God's greater purposes could be jeopardized. There is a mystery to this: how can God demonstrate that He changes His mind in response to our prayers but in another instance assures us that He never changes His mind on the greater scale, the Meta level? Credible theology always has to be worked out from the basis of Biblical revelation. Bearing in mind what we've said about Quantum mechanics, in a typical Biblical way we must simultaneously hold two seemingly contradictory concepts: God is in full control of history, and, at the same time, there is a high degree of human freedom and responsibility that influences history, but which will never derail the ultimate outcome.

Take a look at the book of Esther, one of the most mysterious and fascinating stories in the Bible. It tells the story of a king who insulted his wife while he was drunk and (to cut a long story short) had to find a new wife. The chosen wife happened to be Jewish. At the same time, one of the king's main advisers, Haman, was infuriated by a Jewish man, Mordecai, who refused to bow before Haman because of his ethnic background. Haman was an Agagite, a group that God put under a curse for their attack on the

Israelites long before. So there was more to this than just personal animosity. In revenge, Haman got the king to order the execution of all the Jews in the empire. Just before the massacre was going to take place the king had a sleepless night and asked some of his assistants to read from the historical records of his reign. As they read those to the king they came upon an entry which chronicled a time when Mordecai had saved the king's life. The King discovers that Mordecai was never thanked, so he orders Haman (of all people) to lead Mordecai dressed in royal attire around the capitol on the king's horse while shouting: "This is what the king does to someone he wants to honor." Ironically, Haman had expected to be the person to be honored and would never have dreamed he'd have to honor his mortal enemy. He tells the story to his family who gets the point right away—this is the beginning of the end for Haman. Haman finally discovers that Esther, the king's favorite wife, is Mordecai's niece. When everything is revealed the king decides to execute Haman and makes Mordecai his lead advisor.

The story is full of twists and turns and shows how God, working in the background as an unnoticed film director, does exactly what He wants, but in a way that allows for the mystery of human will and responsibility to coexist. He is, after all, the God who created the mysteries of physics and supra complex ecosystems. He will continue to surprise us, throughout eternity.

THE PROMISE OF JESUS

Jesus told us in Matthew 28 that He has all authority in heaven and on earth, and that His disciples would be serving Him all over the globe, making all nations into His disciples.

He also promised, in Luke 24, after His resurrection, that repentance and forgiveness of sins would be proclaimed to all nations.

The Apostolic Church understood that this was a fulfillment of God's promise to David when He said: "'After this I will return, and I will rebuild the tent of David that has fallen; I will rebuild its ruins, and I will restore it, that the remnant of mankind may seek the Lord, and all the Gentiles who are called by my name, says the Lord, who makes these things known from of old.'" (Acts 15:16–18)

Since we are seeing that God has kept His promises to Abraham in a very literal way, and also that Jesus' promise of the spreading of the Gospel is happening, it should not surprise us that God is at work in all the world to continue to do what He promised, and also increase the speed. But there is more to discover when it comes to the Middle Eastern world. There are some aspects that are especially relevant to the fulfillment of the promises.

THE PROMISE TO ABRAHAM

Isaac was not Abraham's only son—Ishmael was his other. It was through Isaac that the promise of a land, a nation, and the blessing to the nations would come. However, there was also a promise for Ishmael:

God promised both Abraham and Hagar that He would make Ishmael into a great nation (Genesis 16 & 21:8–21). In salvation history there is a big difference between being chosen to be a blessing to the world and being blessed in general.

Abraham's family life was to be complicated. When he and Sarah thought that they would never have any children Sarah suggested that Abraham should have a son for them through Hagar, her Egyptian slave. Notice that there is no criticism in the Bible of Abraham for doing this. When Hagar got pregnant and Sarah started to treat her badly, an angel of the Lord appeared and told Hagar what to name her son and that the Lord had listened to the cries of her son. She also found out that there would be conflict around him and that there would be infighting within his people. On hearing this, Hagar worshiped the Lord and said of Him: "You are a God of seeing" because "Truly here I have seen Him who looks after me."

The Tsunami and What to Expect: Revival in the Muslim World

ISHMAEL'S REBELLION AND SALVATION

Ishmael's descendants, in early times, settled from the eastern border of Egypt across the desert towards the Persian/Arab Gulf and peopled the north and the west of the Arabian peninsula (Gen 25:12–18), today's Saudi Arabia. They have not followed the way of the Lord. On the surface they seem to be one of the more resistant nations to God. But that should not fool us. We can argue that Israel is in the same position and the Bible tells us so, but that does not mean that God is giving up on them. The rebellion of every nation on earth is very real and causes pain and suffering all over the world. However, according to Jesus Christ, God will bring the nations, including Israel and the Arab world, to salvation.

THE ABRAHAM CONNECTION

Is it really happening?

It is extremely difficult to assert the numbers of Arab converts to Jesus Christ. Open conversion is an automatic death sentence in some countries. In others, if detected, conversion means imprisonment, divorce if married, and exclusion from society. To become a Christian can mean losing it all for faith in Jesus Christ.

But still it happens—and on a surprisingly large scale. One of the most effective evangelists to the Arab world is an elderly Coptic priest, Zacharias Boutros. He was forced to emigrate from his home country Egypt to USA because Al-Qaeda once put a bounty of 60 million Canadian dollars to anyone who murdered him—calling him "the world's most wanted infidel."

Boutros has a doctoral degree in Islamic Studies, has written books criticizing Islam, but he is best known for his TV programs that are watched all over the world, notwithstanding having to change TV stations frequently because of threats. Boutros has been called Islam's public enemy No. 1. Some have tried to get him extradited back to Egypt for criticizing Islam, or have threatened to break diplomatic relations with countries that allow broadcasting of his TV programs. He has also been falsely accused of having been excommunicated by the Coptic Church.

Zacharias Boutros's TV programs have been followed by up to 50 million viewers per day. That is an amazing number. A Muslim cleric on Al Jazeera warned recently that there might be as many as 6 million people converted to faith in Christ every year as a result of Zacharias Boutros' ministry. Most of the converts are obviously covert. It is not possible to verify these numbers and they may well be inflated, but they do show the concern of the traditionalists in the region. It points to a possible build up to a tsunami-like cultural earthquake that may come sooner than we expect.

GOD ACTS SOVEREIGNLY

The most common cause for conversions among Muslims to Christ seems, however, to be the sovereign intervention of God Himself. It happens through dreams and visions, a thing that religious fundamentalists and cultural chains cannot control. God is using dreams, visions and the personal testimony of those receiving them in a way that seems to exceed earlier centuries. Communicating through dreams is no new phenomenon—God spoke through them to Abraham, Jacob, Joseph and frequently to others in the New Testament, so it should not come as a great surprise.

A friend of ours is a Christian pastor in the Middle East. One day he heard a furious Muslim lady shouting outside their house, adjacent to the church: "Christians are cowards, Christians are cowards. . .!" He ran outside to ask her why she was so angry, and she was more than happy to tell him. During the night Jesus had appeared to her in a dream and told her to go to a church, get a Bible and read it to know how to believe in Him. Early in the morning she went to one church after another (this is in a mixed area, but conversions are still forbidden) but no one dared to give her a Bible for fear that she was a spy. Our friend is not easily scared and he invited her to the church, gave a her a Bible and explained the Gospel about Jesus to her.

The Tsunami and What to Expect: Revival in the Muslim World

This true story gives us some insight into the problem of knowing how many Arab Muslims have turned to Christ. The traditional churches live under the threat of persecution most of the time for just being Christians, even though the members often come from other ethnic identities. They are therefore often hesitant to welcome Muslim converts. There is no real freedom of religion in most of the Middle East countries. There are attempts to create peaceful coexistence but on the condition of absolutely no evangelism or conversions. So any Muslim convert is by default forced to stay within their own community and relate to small groups that have very limited interactions, often via a few underground leaders.

It is difficult to present any credible, Western-style statistics that could give a precise number of how many former Muslims live covertly in Islam-dominated countries in the Middle East and North Africa. All that can be said is that the reports of people meeting Jesus personally are coming from all over the area. Many call themselves "Muslims who believe in Jesus," not in Muhammad. They meet in small groups, witness by asking questions from the Quran, and take a high risk by sharing Christ and by being baptized or by baptizing someone. To give a picture, let me share what a Christian leader told us about what happens in Cairo alone: he estimates that there are one thousand converts per day. That's in one city, in one nation. No organization is in charge of the enormous movement to Christ; no church or leader is or could even be orchestrating it. And no one knows how to stop it. A credible source estimates that 350 million people live as secret Christians in the Muslim world. This is not even thanks to ISIS or the reaction to other extremist groups that propelled many to abandon Islam, even if that of course contributes. It is a result of God's sovereign action in history and it follows the same pattern as we see in the Book of Acts and in the early Church.

As far as we can tell, these large-scale conversions because of dreams did not begin to happen until sometime in the 1900s. The scale of it is new and should be a sobering revelation to all world leaders.

WHAT THIS MEANS

Islam is the ideological fabric that holds the Muslim-majority countries together. Though there are many variations of Islam and the intensity of its adherents vary a lot, religion is a determining identity factor even in the more secular areas. Once this fabric is perceived as being under threat there will be severe turmoil that will affect not only the region, but also other parts of the world, and the West will certainly feel the fury of the ones that stand to lose the most because of the change.

MODERN COMMUNICATIONS ENCOURAGE PEOPLE TO QUESTION ISLAM

We hear a lot of claims that Christianity and Islam are very similar. We must not let ourselves be fooled by such statements. Western politicians and quite a few religious leaders realize they need to say this for what they believe is the good of their nations. It does require effort to distinguish between good, law-abiding Muslims who want to live their lives in peace, and the radical and extremist groups that seem to find their true identity in domineering and wiping out anyone who won't submit. Similarly, it takes effort and courage to look at some important differences between Islam and the historic Christian faith. There are obvious and well-known theological differences, but we will look at that one basic difference which makes true dialogue difficult and which will be a critical factor in the future demise of Islam as it is understood today.

This basic difference is the relationship between the Qur'an and Muhammad, on the one hand, and Jesus and the Bible, on the other.

In Islam, the book of Qur'an is thought to have been delivered from heaven by an angel who dictated its content directly to the prophet Muhammad. With that view of the Qur'an it makes absolute perfect sense to claim that the Qur'an cannot be subject to questioning or historical analysis. It bears absolute authority in itself. Any attempt to ask embarrassing questions is almost blasphemous. Muhammad, although highly regarded, is understood as a prophetic messenger who was used to give the Qur'an to the world and to provide the basic interpretation.

The Christian faith believes the other way around. Jesus Christ is the one who came from heaven. He is the Word of God, and the Bible witnesses about Him. The Bible is absolutely true, and Jesus Himself taught that it has full authority. Since it is God's message that He has spoken through the prophets, everything it promises will happen. That sounds similar to the way orthodox Muslims view the Qur'an, but there are major differences that will lead in opposite directions.

The Bible is a collection of books, written under the inspiration of God's Spirit. It was given throughout history and its message is intertwined with history. God spoke and acted and one sure sign of its Divine origin was that what it foretold would happen. A believer can therefore be certain of the Bible's credibility by comparing what was said with what happened. Jesus exemplified this principle when He told His disciples that He must go to Jerusalem to be handed over to the God-rejecting authorities, be crucified and then resurrected on the third day, so that the Scriptures should be fulfilled. Being ready to die in order to be resurrected according to the Scriptures is the highest measure of trust in the veracity of God's promises. Living this way is the only way in which one can know that the Bible is absolutely true. Therefore, it is not a problem to ask questions about the veracity of the Bible. It is actually necessary in order to build up one's faith toward complete trust in God's character. But it is also necessary to see Jesus as the model of how to trust the Bible. Honest, even daring questions, will increase faith, not undermine it. We understand that the Bible is true because in it we have age-old testimonies of God's absolute faithfulness. It is a faith based on seeing how God has acted and is acting in history. It is not blind faith.

A religion that presupposes blind faith is bound to collapse in this globally intertwined world. Faith that will last is built on revelation that is integrated with the created reality and is open to the possibility of being verified. There is so much information readily available, with technology and the sciences opening up an even further hitherto unknown and even unthinkable world. Both rigid religion and rigid secularism are therefore bound to collapse, and that will probably happen within the next 25 years. This tsunami of new insights is one of the factors behind the rise of radical Islam, and it will probably increase before it leads to its collapse one way or another.

SOCIAL PROBLEMS

Another indicator of the fissuring in the Middle East and Islam are the serious social problems that many experience within that world. START 2015 statistics highlighted that while the Arab region is home to 5% of the world's population, the region is linked to 45% of global terrorist attacks, 68% of the world's battle-related deaths and 57% of the world's refugees. According to World Bank statistics, the unemployment level for persons between 15–24 is twice as high as the global average.

The START statistics go some length in shedding light on social problems which have created the societal volatility we're witnessing today. Governments in the region have struggled with mixed success to address these problems which have spread to affect the wider region as well as potentially posing a threat to the entire world. It is more than a little naive to seek an explanation for the problems in simple economic or religious terms—these are deeply complex problems. Nonetheless, the facts gleaned from the studies point towards a perfect storm created by rigid religion, fearful and authoritarian rulers operating in a context of serious economic pressures.

Few if any of the regional regimes are perceived by the more fundamentalist citizens as legitimate. Some countries are ruled by ruthless and corrupt regimes who see it is their role to perpetuate their own power, while others desperately try to out-maneuver the more extreme political-religious movements like the Muslim Brotherhood in Sunni dominated areas. The Brotherhood won a recent election in Egypt and was quickly overthrown; they seem

The Tsunami and What to Expect: Revival in the Muslim World

to have won an election in Morocco where the constitution will make it virtually impossible for them to rule, and the movement is outlawed in many places. The lack of freedom of expression creates mistrust and even hatred towards the rulers. It also fuels even more extreme feelings directed against the Western powers who support such authoritarian regimes.

Since there is little scope within the culture and religion to question religious or cultural factors the problems cannot be addressed fully. The only option is to pass the blame: the 'logical' and necessary causes must come from the outside, such as the Western world or Israel.

But as we have seen, something significant is happening that regional political powers, religious elites or secular Western politicians are unable to perceive. There is a remarkable underground change taking place and I believe that this is for the fulfillment of God's ancient promises.

Although Islam is divided, and there is a lot of infighting, it is the cohesive factor in the Middle East, and if its overall influence wanes, the system will collapse. The consequences of that will meet extreme and strong resistance from both religious and political leaders, and may well be more chaotic than was the fall of the Soviet Union. One thing is certain: it will change the geopolitical situation in the region dramatically and impact the economies that are dependent on that region's stability.

A Christ-empowered movement will most likely lead to increased persecution of Christians in the region. It may also fuel increased persecution of Christians in other parts of the world, as the movement creates political uncertainty and endangers business. It will most certainly heighten the political and military pressure on Israel, since some of the political leaders in the region, especially Iran, seem to believe that by obliterating Israel they will "prove" the Bible wrong. Those who harbor such ideas have obviously not read the book of Esther very closely.

God and the Spiritual Tsunami

AT THE END OF THE DAY, THERE IS NOTHING THAT CAN OVERTHROW GOD'S PLANS.

None of us can predict how all this will influence the rest of the world, except to say that it will have an enormous impact and probably create even more political and economic instability. But as Christians, having read the Bible, we expect great and global blessings; that is, of course, in the long run. Be assured that it will happen. God's promise was made more than 4000 years ago, Jesus prepared us for it 2000 years ago, and it is now taking place right before our eyes, if we care to look.

Chapter 9

The Tsunami and What to Expect: Israel's Conversion and Our Response

In this chapter I aim to show that:

1. There will also be a powerful era of conversion to Christ of Israel
2. God has planned salvation history in a way that ensures that will happen
3. Believers are called to pray, live and express their faith in view of this future development

REVIVAL WITH CONSEQUENCES

Imagine the political, economic and military consequences of a continued and deepened Christ-movement in the Middle East. Then consider a next step: a vast majority of the nation of Israel discover and recognize that Jesus really is the Messiah/the Christ. It would cause bewilderment in Europe and the United States and create a need to reset international relations. This may sound far-fetched, I know, but the seemingly impossible process of change has already begun, and the argument for why it will continue and deepen are based on Biblical, historically verifiable facts.

God and the Spiritual Tsunami

Not only should we expect a great and continued revival in the Middle East, but another amazing Biblical promise is that all Israel will one day come to faith in Jesus Christ. In Romans chapters 9–12 God has revealed His plan to make this happen. When we superimpose those chapters on earlier correlating Biblical promises it points to a global change that will have colossal impact.

There are many theories of how this national conversion might come about. Some could be pointing in the right direction, while others are pure speculation and of very limited value. Good theology is based on a disciplined presentation of revealed facts. While it might be tempting to paint a fuller picture of the future than the Bible gives us, it is counterproductive and will create more cynicism than faith and trust. To illustrate this, recall how at the time when Jesus Christ was born there were many who claimed to 'know' what was about to happen. Based on limited information, they predicted that the Romans were going to be defeated and that Israel was going to become the religious, political and financial center of the world with the Messiah ruling from his throne in Jerusalem. Sure, there was some truth in these speculations—even Jesus' disciples embraced them—but at the same time they missed the mark by a mile. The historical development was far more rich and complex and far greater in its scope than the early predictors had foreseen. They hadn't anticipated that the change the Messiah would bring wouldn't primarily be a superficial change in the political landscape, but a deep and profound change of the human heart. Similarly, we must be careful and always open to learning, reflecting and reevaluating as we think about the conversion of Israel. In that spirit, let me throw in a caveat: some of the contemporary theories presented today might be perfectly accurate, but we cannot be sure until they happen. Here is the exciting thing: the Biblical facts will be realized in greater depth, with more far-reaching consequences and stretching personal challenges than we are able to imagine. The way God works things out will always blow our minds and challenge our preconceived ideas.

Again, the clearest Biblical teaching on this subject is found in Romans chapters 9–12. Let us look at the main ideas of the text step by step.

HOW PAUL THOUGHT

The content of these chapters is very foreign to our customary way of thinking, but once we come to grips with what they are telling us, they are actually a great help to see what salvation history accomplishes. To a secular Western mind the text may be among the most difficult ones in the Bible. Taken out of its Biblical context some teaching on it has generated disunity, infighting and division among equally committed Christians. I love taking the bull by the horns! I feel confident there is a way to understand the Biblical writers and learn from them because God meant for us to understand, with His help.

Paul was a genuine Hebrew thinker. He was highly educated and wrote his letters to the churches in Greek. However, being a Jew, his intrinsic thought pattern was Hebrew/Semitic. That Hebrew way of thinking meant, among other things, that he based his teaching on what God has revealed through the prophets in the Scriptures, and then sought the outworking of those promises in history. This is one of the significant aspects of Biblical revelation, and one that differs from other religions. The Bible is not just a book of great, inspiring ideas but an integrated revelation of what God has said and what He has done in history. There is a correlation between what He said and what happens, and, therefore, also what will happen. In the beginning He said "Let there be. . .." He told Noah of the Flood and then sent the flood. He told Abraham to follow Him and promised Him a son, a nation, a land and that he would be a blessing to all nations. He told Moses to free His people and then led them out of bondage. He told Joshua to march around Jericho until the walls fell; they did. He warned Israel and Judah of upcoming captivities, and, of course, that the Messiah would be raised on the third day. The proof that all this was true was that it was verifiable: it actually happened. A true prophet was

God and the Spiritual Tsunami

recognized by the fact that what he said actually happened. Otherwise he was a false prophet. Simple.

Since this was Paul's way of thinking, he had a worldview that would not put any limitation on what God was able to do or not do. What to us might seem like confusing contradictions—when he for example teaches about God's sovereign choices and our human responsibility to believe, pray and witness—is perfectly fine with Paul, who builds his teaching on what God has said and done rather than on a Western, linear way of thinking. He wrote in Greek, but he did not intend to convey Greek ideas. His reference point was not his immediate, limited experience. His reference point was Scripture. If this idea raises objections in you—and I can see why it would—let me offer an illustration of how two things can be true, while at the same time seem mutually exclusive.

PHYSICS HIGHLIGHTS OUR DILEMMA IN A BEAUTIFUL WAY

Take classical physics that we see in action every day. With help from men like Newton and Einstein, a lot of it—but not all—makes perfect sense. It looks logical in the straightforward way our brains appreciate. But don't be fooled—there is more to the story.

Enter quantum theory: it is an overarching theory of modern physics discovered in the 1900s that describes how matter and energy behave on the atomic and subatomic level. Some of what it reveals is clearly counter-intuitive and frustratingly mind-bending, but if you persist in reading these few lines I hope you will feel rewarded.

Quantum theory is the theoretical basis of modern physics that explains the nature and behavior of matter and energy on the atomic and subatomic level. The nature and behavior of matter and energy at that level is sometimes referred to as quantum physics and quantum mechanics.

> Try to visualize this: within this theory of physics, elementary particles can both behave like particles or waves

The Tsunami and What to Expect: Israel's Conversion

depending on the conditions. This phenomenon is called "wave-particle duality." Or think about the uncertainty principle, which tells us that we cannot simultaneously measure particles position and momentum at the same time. The more precise one value is, the more flawed the other will be.

Then we have one of the most challenging ideas: Niels Bohr, a Danish physicist, claimed that he discovered that a particle might not even exist until it is measured or observed in some way. Imagine that. How can something not exist until it's been spotted?

If you think this is nonsense and impossible you are in good company. Albert Einstein spent years trying to disprove this theory. However, it has since been verified, and if you own a mobile phone you are using a gadget that is built on the principle of quantum mechanics.

Not only is all this logically bewildering. It looks like our brains were not created to understand this intuitively. We are bound to rely on experiments and mathematics in order to use it. But there is even more to the story. Hold on to your chair.

There is today no known theory to explain the relationship between classical physics (what we would see as every-day logical physics) and quantum physics. It is as if they exist in separate realities, although our lives depend on them both. There continue to be attempts to bridge the two realities, but no attempt to date has fully succeeded.

Let's go back to the Bible and Paul's teaching: behind all reality is God. He created the world, which means that He planned each aspect of it in minute detail. That includes the realities we are aware of but cannot explain.

When we read what Paul is writing we must remember that He, as a Hebrew scholar, was fully aware that God's absolute knowledge is immensely higher than any human knowledge.

In 1 Corinthians Paul wrote that God's "foolishness" (if there is such a thing) is wiser than men's wisdom. Paul is expressing the immensity of God's knowledge. The consequence of this is immediate: the only things we really can know about God (except that He exists and by definition is almighty) is what God Himself has revealed about Himself in creation, through the prophets in the Bible and through His incarnate revelation in Jesus Christ—the Word, who is God, and who became man (John 1:1–3). As for the rest, we do well if we recognize that the One who thought out and created this world, which is far richer, greater and more complex than we can comprehend, knows more than we do. He who created the laws of physics as well as quantum physics fully understands the relation between the two and can do things that are fully rational to Him, while we will probably have to wait for heaven to have it explained.

I hope we are now ready to look at Paul's teaching in Romans 9–12, bearing in mind Paul's perspective: what God has promised, He will deliver.

ALL ISRAEL WILL COME TO FAITH IN JESUS CHRIST

Most Israelis are today secular, but this will one day change dramatically. When Paul actualizes the promise in Romans 11:26 he most certainly means the entire ethnic nation of Israel—he is not referring both to Jews and Gentiles. In the sentence immediately before the promise he has said that the fullness of the Gentiles will come to salvation, so he must be referring only to ethnic Jews in the following sentence.

Israel's conversion will probably not look like anything we can envisage. It will certainly not be a copy of any Western or Eastern church tradition or a reformation of Israel's own religious traditions. It will be the result of a whole nation being reborn in a short period of time. Look at the emerging churches in China or the Muslim world, and you will see what I mean.

The important point to take away is that it will happen one day as a fulfillment of God's promise to Abraham. This includes not only becoming a nation, but also that the nation promised would continue to be a blessing to all nations (which is being fulfilled through the spread of the Gospel). Not only will there be an

The Tsunami and What to Expect: Israel's Conversion

Abrahamic nation, but an Abrahamic nation that knows God the way Abraham did.

I find it quite surprising that Israel's conversion is an issue of debate in the first place. Jesus authorized His followers to make all nations His disciples, which must mean that the nation of Israel also will come to faith in Jesus Christ on a scale much greater than we've seen so far. So far in history, Israel has never claimed to be a Christian nation.

ISRAEL AS A NATION REFUSED TO BELIEVE IN CHRIST

In Romans chapter 10 Paul teaches that Israel chose to reject the Gospel when it was presented to them by Jesus Christ. There were two main reasons for the rejection. The first and most serious one was that Israel acted and thought like all other nations. They had already rejected the revelation that God had given them and their actions followed this thinking. Their religious formalities were different from the ones in other cultures, but the end result was the same. Jesus Christ criticized that maneuver harshly and exposed it as hypocrisy. When the people were invited to enter the Kingdom of God they understood that they would have to change both their world view and behavior, and they chose to reject the invitation. Not that Israel's hypocrisy was worse than that of other nations—for all the reasons given in previous chapters, other nations would have done the same given the same circumstances—but Israel's strategic role and opportunity at that time was unique and therefore the consequences of that move were more far-reaching.

The second reason for their rejection was that, when Jesus came to them, He did not fit their expectation of what the Christ would do. They already thought they were on God's side and that now was the time for freedom from the occupation forces.

Changing the political landscape was not Jesus' primary agenda. Instead, it became obvious that Christ had come to fulfill (and thereby end) some of the most cherished traditions of their culture (legalism) and die as a sacrifice for the sins of the people and the world. They furiously resisted that re-writing of their expectations.

But here God revealed His Divine wisdom in a way that has bewildered people through the ages. He offered salvation by faith in Jesus Christ to all the Gentile nations, with the dual purpose of blessing them while preparing Israel for a time of national conversion and restoration. Salvation is always undeserved and the result of God's mercy.

GOD OFFERED SALVATION TO THE GENTILE NATIONS

There was an old Biblical promise that God would make the Gentiles a part of His people. That was difficult to comprehend at the time of Jesus Christ when Israel was occupied by the Romans and had suffered much under various Gentile rules. The Jews also, rightly, saw themselves as God's special people and many looked down on the Gentiles, wanting to have as little to do with them as possible.

The Gentiles in Israel, on the other hand, looked down on the Jews. They chose not to fit into the larger, dominating culture. They preferred to befriend their own, and absolutely refused to participate in anything that they perceived as a foreign religion. There were some who respected that and read enough from the Old Testament to cause them to convert from their pagan religions, but they were in the minority.

After the church was born things changed rapidly, but initially the early Church had no vision of reaching the Gentiles. They were just discovering a new faith in Christ and working to live this out as faithful Jews, as they imagined they were supposed to do. However, God had other plans. Even though He had revealed them a long time ago, it would take Divine intervention to direct the Church to do what He had told them to do. On the day of Pentecost when the Holy Spirit filled the disciples they spontaneously preached the Gospel in many different languages. There is no doubt that the Christians were doing God's will—they were

The Tsunami and What to Expect: Israel's Conversion

assured of His favor through the signs and wonders that followed them.

After the stoning of Stephen, the church in Jerusalem was scattered, and one of the believers, the evangelist Philip, preached in Samaria (a despised mixed blood community). The Apostles Peter and John travelled there and gave their approval to what was going on. That breakthrough came as a result of strong persecution. It even led to (with the clear guidance of the Holy Spirit) the conversion of an Ethiopian official who happen to travel through the area.

That was just the beginning. The book of Acts reveals another storyline that runs alongside the historical recording of events: of how the Gospel came to the Gentiles. It begins with a devout and totally committed Jewish leader, Saul, who was converted by the direct intervention of God.

Saul hated Christians and was persecuting them when God stopped him in his tracks, told him what to do and indicated to some early Christians that God had a distinct plan for Saul. That was one step in the development. Saul later becomes known as Paul, the Apostle.

While the Christians continued to preach to and relate to their own ethnic groups, God intervened again by telling a Roman officer named Cornelius that He was sending the Apostle Peter to him so he could hear the Gospel and be saved. At the same time, He gave Peter a vision that showed him how God viewed some of the Jewish traditions he followed, and instructed him to go to Cornelius and lead him to faith in Jesus Christ. This was wonderful and according to God's plan with history, but Peter's friends were not happy. They questioned his visit and had to be convinced by hearing that the Holy Spirit had filled the Gentiles. Then they accepted that this event truly was from God.

It still took some time before the real breakthrough happened. Some Jewish Christians did preach to the Gentiles, but most did not. Not until some of them met in Antioch to pray and God ordered them to send Paul, the former persecutor, and his friend Barnabas to preach to all the nations.

God and the Spiritual Tsunami

From the beginning the Bible shows that preaching to the Gentiles was at the heart of God's plan. This was reinforced by Jesus in His last instructions to His disciples, what we now call the 'Great Commission'. As the Apostles were forced to defend their actions and teachings, they referred to what God already spoken through His prophets in e.g. Isaiah 45:21; 49:6 and Amos 9:11–12. It was the Apostle Paul who shortly afterwards took things one step further when he Scripturally defended the Gentiles' right to the Gospel without having to submit to the Jewish law as well. (A note: This does not mean that the early Church adapted the message to the times, as some people argue we should do today. They discovered and adapted themselves to what God already had revealed in the Scriptures.)

This development not only brought the Gospel to the Gentile nations, but led the newly birthed Church to discover the innermost parts of the Christian Gospel: justification by faith alone. Jesus' payment on the cross was enough—nothing else was needed to be right with God again. Yes, Jewish Christians were to keep the Jewish law that God had given them to protect their identity as Israelites, while understanding that keeping the law was not going to save them. Salvation came through believing in Jesus. Believing was itself a gift of the Holy Spirit and was necessary in order to live in true fellowship with God. That was what the Apostles taught and how they lived. It was to profoundly influence the earliest Church's understanding of the Gospel.

TWO REASONS FOR PREACHING THE GOSPEL TO THE NATIONS

So far we have seen how God's plan to save all nations was only gradually uncovered by the first Christians. The process of how they got there was led by the Holy Spirit, and by His help they discovered what had been foretold in the Scriptures. It may seem obvious to us, but, to be fair, it is not easy to imagine something you're not expecting to see. Based on that understanding the Church increasingly preached to the Gentiles. The rejection by the

The Tsunami and What to Expect: Israel's Conversion

nation of Israel was no longer a surprise but an indicator about what to do next.

Then comes the twist. Yes, God wants to save all nations. He had already indicated that in His promise to Abraham, through the Prophets and in Jesus' Great Commission. There's also more to it: His plan includes using the blessing He shows to the Gentiles to bring Israel to faith. This is how Paul visualizes it: ". . .I am speaking to you Gentiles. Inasmuch then as I am an apostle to the Gentiles, I magnify my ministry in order somehow to make my fellow Jews jealous, and thus save some of them." (Romans 11:13-14) Paul writes this a purpose of his ministry. It is not just a pious hope. When the Israelis see the real power of God they will be attracted to it. Paul's ministry did lead to the conversion of many Jews, while it led to increased resistance from others.

The lesson is that it takes a vital, dynamic, apostolic-like church to attract the Jewish nation to faith in Christ. Arguments won't do it. Neither religious outliers, or churches focused primarily on institutional goals or ceremonial formalities, have contributed to it.

I, for one, believe that the emerging, underground church in the Middle East will be an important factor. The dynamics of that divinely and Spirit-led movement (which displays important characteristics of the Church in Acts), and the impact which it will have on the region, may well be the force that prepares Israel for its next divine intervention, finally accomplishing Paul's dream.

Reason one: God will in no way annul His promise to Abraham

As we have seen, there is one unyielding reason why we can be so sure of the conversion of Israel: because of God's covenantal promise to Abraham. By the time of Paul it was clear to anyone who cared to watch history that God intended to keep His promises, and not even Israel's own rejection of God's ways would stop that. Today after the end of the diaspora that argument is even stronger.

In Paul's theology it would be absolutely inconceivable that God would revoke what He promised. There were times when Israel bore the consequences of its rebellion: time and time again during the time of the Judges, when the country was divided, and during the Babylonian captivity. But none of those times brought an end to God's plans for Israel. The captivities were means to bring the people back to their senses and back to God. The aim was the same with the long diaspora after the destruction of Jerusalem.

Paul reminds us that because of God's own character His callings and gifts cannot be revoked. It is in that context that he writes about the conversion of all Israel.

Reason two: Since God used the unbelief of Israel to bless the Gentiles, how much more will He not use the future belief of Israel to bless the entire world

God's promise to Abraham 4,000 years ago was that his descendants would be a blessing to all nations. The most important aspect of that promise has already taken place since the coming of Jesus Christ: He is the descendant of Abraham that changed the status of mankind's relationship to God. Paul does, however, anticipate one more chapter of the story that will be seen after the conversion of Israel. The more of the presence of God that is manifest on earth, the more blessing, wholeness and joy there will be. Joseph, Daniel and Mordecai & Esther are reminders of this.

In Romans chapter 12 he therefore challenges the Gentile Christians both to change their way of thinking and to live according to their new understanding of God's dealing in history.

He begins this part of his letter with a challenge that is based on what he just had written:

> Verse 1 begins: "Therefore" (which means "Because of this...") use your bodies to serve God the way He intends for you. That means that we should: not live according to the standards of this world, but by seeing and understanding who God is and what He is up to, be changed, letting our minds be renewed by this revelation in a way

that God accepts, and obviously, from the context, let our lifestyle speak of the reality of the Gospel.

There are at least two takeaways from this teaching. The first one is that God is faithful and will surely do what He promised Abraham and what He, in Jesus, reiterated: that all nations, including Israel, will be made disciples.

The second is that Gentile Christians need to think and live with God's perspective on history. Since God is about to do all the great things, such as leading all nations to faith in Jesus, it is necessary for us to live fully committed lives, to let our minds be renewed by Him and not to take our clues for living from the world around us.

In some mysterious way, our lives are intertwined with God's great purposes. Paul, who wrote this and knew that He would have to wait for all Israel to be saved, did pray for His people and so longed for their conversion that he was willing to be lost himself if it would help them. Our prayers for the world, our own nation or Israel's, might not be answered instantly. Our committed Christian lifestyle might not be appreciated by all right away. But what is far more important is that our lives are a part of God's way of bringing salvation to the world. The story of John Hus is an illustration of this and a challenge to follow Paul's and his example.

These future changes will contribute to more church growth and intensified resistance than we have ever seen before. We are already now called to be a part of God's plan by living in such a way that the Kingdom of God is clearly shown.

www.ingramcontent.com/pod-product-compliance
Lightning Source LLC
Chambersburg PA
CBHW071439160426
43195CB00013B/1963